For Dave
Dance with Paisley

Blessings!

Ginger

Dancing on Daddy's Feet

and
Other Stories of God's Love

By Ginger LaGrone Tucker

© 2007 by Ginger Tucker
Printed in the United States of America
ISBN 0-971-9746-7-8

Published by:
GKT Publishing
GKT Consulting, Inc.
Amarillo, Texas
806-353-7291
www.gingertucker.com

Printed by Cenveo Printing in Amarillo, Texas

Dedication

To Him who is able to do exceeding abundantly beyond all that we ask or think, according to the power that works within us,
To Him be the glory in the church and in Christ Jesus, to all generations forever and ever. Amen.

Ephesians 3:20-21

Contents

LOVE - JOY - PEACE

PATIENCE - KINDNESS - GOODNESS

FAITHFULNESS - GENTLENESS - SELF-CONTROL

Format

Following each short story is a section called, *Thinking About It,* designed to help the reader apply the lessons personally. Each chapter has some or all of the following features:

- **?** **Your Thoughts** will lead you to think about, meditate on, or journal your thoughts about the principles and lessons from the story.
- **Go Deeper** will challenge you to get more out of suggested Bible passages and encourage you to memorize related scriptures.
- **†** **So What?** Will provide the opportunity for you to apply the lessons to your thinking and actions. What do you want to remember? What difference does this make to you? What will you do?
- **Study Session** will expand your knowledge of the Biblical principles beneath the stories. I suggest that you read the Bible passages and make notes as you study. You may also find it helpful to use commentaries, dictionaries, and other translations of the Bible as you study. As you study, pray and ask God to reveal His Word to you—He will.
- **Praying** begins with a scriptural prayer with space for your personal addition.

Dancing on Daddy's Feet and Other Stories of God's Love

LOVE ~ JOY ~ PEACE

Dancing on Daddy's Feet

Do You Know Bailey's Jesus?

A Picture of the Father

Granny's Grace

But when the Holy Spirit controls our lives, he will produce this kind of fruit in us: love, joy, peace, patience, kindness, goodness, faithfulness, gentleness, and self-control.
Galatians 5:22 NLT

Chapter 1

Dancing on Daddy's Feet

*Let them praise His name with dancing…*Psalm 149:3

Some of my favorite childhood memories are when my parents would move the coffee table out of the way, roll up the rug and dance in our living room. With Marty Robbins or Elvis on the turntable, they danced. Sometimes we children would just watch, wide-eyed and admiring, as our parents laughed and moved with such graceful precision. Sometimes we danced alongside them flailing arms and legs, trying to imitate. Sometimes, my favorite times, we got to dance with them. Daddy would pick us up in his strong arms, holding us securely as he and Mother danced. We would all cry out for our turns. "Me next! Me next!" We wished it would never end.

As I got older, I learned to dance on Daddy's feet. On my Daddy's feet, I didn't need to look down and watch my own feet; I didn't need to plan my steps because he was in control. He was dancing; he was leading.

Sometimes as we danced, I would decide I could do it on my own and would step off his feet to try my own dance. I couldn't do it – I kept stepping on his feet and tripping myself. Daddy would say, "Honey, stay on my feet, and let me lead. Let me show you." We could even master some fancy moves, as long as he led. All I had to do was to gaze up in his loving, laughing eyes. Then I could say, "Look at me! I'm dancing!" As long as I stayed on Daddy's feet, I was dancing; as long as I focused on Daddy's face, I was dancing.

How like our journey through this dance of life. Sometimes my Heavenly Father has held me up securely and tightly in His strong arms. I've been through those times and in places where the only hope and comfort was in my Father's arms—showered with love and mercy—protected from the evil one. Sometimes I'm stronger, and I dance on His feet. But, always, always, He has to lead…when I try to go it on my own, I mess up. It's moving, but it's not The Dance. Without His guidance, I cannot make it. Even when I feel strong and mature I want to dance in His arms, moving and following His subtle lead.

As you go through your dance of life, remember that we cannot do it on our own. Without Him we are nothing. (John 15:5) And, with Him all things are possible. (Luke 1:37, Matthew 19:26) Stay on your Father's feet. Gaze into His loving face. Let Him lead you through the dance. He alone knows the way.

I want every day I have left to be days of dancing on my Father's feet, under His power and guidance, listening to His loving voice say, "Child, let me lead. '**I am the Way, the Truth, and The Life**.'" John 14:6

Psalm 150

Praise God in His heavenly dwelling; praise Him in his mighty heaven!
Praise Him for His mighty works; praise His unequaled greatness!
Praise him with a blast of the trumpet; praise Him with the lyre and harp!
Praise Him with the tambourine and dancing; praise Him with stringed instruments and flutes!
Praise Him with a clash of cymbals; praise him with loud clanging cymbals.
Let everything that lives sing praises to the Lord! Praise the Lord!
New Living Translation

Thinking About It

? Your Thoughts:

1. Describe the times when our heavenly Father has carried you, held you, and/or led you.

2. How does Jesus use the example of a vine and branches in John 14 to explain our relationship with Him?

Go Deeper

Read Psalm 27, 100, and 139. Focus on praising God for His protection and provision. Look for promises to claim.

Select five verses to commit to memory.

† So What?

What do you want to remember from the story? What difference does this make to you? What will you do?

_____

_____

_____

Study Session

Write your thoughts about God's love, protection, and guidance after reading the following:

Nehemiah 8:10

Psalm 23:2-3

Psalm 30:11-12

Psalm 25:4-11

Psalm 61:2

Psalm 66:1-4

Psalm 81:1-3

Psalm 95:1-3

Psalm 98:1,4-6

Psalm 100

Proverbs 6:21-22

Matthew 11:25-30

Colossians 3:12-17

🕊 **Praying** (from Psalm 108:1,3)

My heart is steadfast, O God; I will sing, I will sing praises, even with my soul. I will give thanks to Thee, O Lord, among the peoples; and I will sing praises to Thee among the nations.

_____

_____

_____

_____

Chapter 2

Do You Know Bailey's Jesus?

O Lord, our Lord, How majestic is Thy name in all the earth,
Who hast displayed Thy splendor above the heavens!
From the mouth of infants and nursing babes Thou hast established strength.
Psalm 8:1-2

God recently allowed me to see Jesus through the eyes of someone seeing Him for the first time. Having the advantage of knowing how The Story ends, we can easily forget the cost of our redemption and the love of our Savior. We get so caught up in shopping, parties, Santa and all the holidays trappings that we miss the Message; we miss the Messiah.

Every year we attend a local church Christmas pageant, telling the story of Jesus from His birth through His resurrection. It is a spectacular event, with live animals, awesome special effects, and realistic sets. Dozens of cast members portray angels, shepherds, priests, and peasants using the entire auditorium to reenact the story. The audience turns, straining to see, lifting children in the air, as from the rear of the huge auditorium the exotic magi appear in brilliant colors riding on llamas or carried by servants, descending the steps in pomp and majesty. Roman soldiers look huge and menacing in their crimson costumes and makeup. The angelic host is breathtaking, hanging suspended in the heavens.

Of all the years we have attended, one stands out indelibly in my heart. It was the year we took our then three-year-old granddaughter, Bailey, who loves Jesus. She was mesmerized throughout the entire play, not just watching, but involved as if she were a player. She watched as Joseph and Mary travel to Bethlehem and was thrilled when she saw the baby Jesus in His mother's arms.

When Jesus, on a young donkey, descended the steps from the back of the auditorium, depicting His triumphal entry into Jerusalem, Bailey grew ecstatic. As he neared our aisle, Bailey began jumping up and down, screaming, "Jesus, Jesus! There's Jesus!" Not just saying the words, but exclaiming the words with every fiber of her being. She alternated between screaming His name and hugging us. "It's Jesus. Look!" I thought she might actually pass out.

Tears filled my eyes as I looked at Jesus through the eyes of a child in love with Him, seeing Him for the first time. How like the blind beggar screaming out in reckless abandon, "Jesus, Jesus!", afraid he might miss Him, not caring what others thought. (Mark 10:46-52) It was a true delight watching her watching Him.

But, then came the arrest scene. On stage, the soldiers shoved and slapped Jesus as they moved Him from the Garden of Gethsemane to Pilate. The sound of whips and slaps reverberated. Bailey stood and responded with terror and anger as if she were in the crowd of women. "Stop it!" she screamed. "Bad soldiers! Stop it!" As I watched her reaction, I panicked. I wished we had talked to her before the play. I realized she didn't know how the story ends. "Bailey, it's okay. They are just pretending."

"They are hurting Jesus!" Bailey screamed, "Stop it!" She stood in her seat reacting to each and every move on the stage.

People around us at first smiled at her reaction, thinking, "How cute." But it wasn't cute; it was a child who knew only that her Jesus, who Loves the Little Children, was being hurt. Her world was crumbling. Isn't that what those first disciples must have felt and Mary, too? I began to notice that the people around us had ceased smiling and had begun watching her watch Him, almost as if they were ashamed not to. In a most powerful scene, the soldiers led Jesus carrying the cross down the steps of the auditorium from the back...yelling, whipping, cursing at Jesus, who is bloodied and beaten. Bailey hysterically pleaded, "Stop it! Soldiers! Stop it!"

She must have been wondering why all these people did nothing. Distraught, she then began to cry instead of scream. "Jesus, Oh, Jesus!" People all around us began to weep as we all watched this devoted little disciple see her Jesus beaten and killed as those first century disciples had. "Why doesn't someone do something?" I will never forget the face of the gentleman in front of us as he sat watching Bailey with tears streaming down his face.

Going back and forth between her mother's lap and mine, she was not to be comforted. We kept reassuring, "Bailey, it's okay. Jesus is going to be okay.

These are just people pretending to be soldiers and Jesus." She looked at me like I was crazy. "Jesus…" she cried. In my lap, we talked through the cross and burial. "Watch, Bailey, watch for Jesus!"

At last the tomb trembled and lightening flashed as the stone rolled away. A million-person-superbowl-touchdown-cheer couldn't come close to matching this little one's reaction to the resurrection. First with wide-eyed wonder, then sheer joy, pointing and jumping, she proclaimed, "Jesus! He's okay! Mommy, it's Jesus! Look! He's okay!" People all around us cheered!

I prayed that Bailey wouldn't be traumatized by this event, but that she would remember it. I shall never forget it. I shall never forget seeing Jesus' suffering, crucifixion, and resurrection through the eyes of an innocent child.

Following the pageant the actors all assembled in the foyer to be greeted by the audience. As we passed by some of the soldiers, Bailey lashed out, "Bad soldier, don't you hurt Jesus." The actor who portrayed Jesus was some distance away surrounded by well-wishers and friends. Bailey broke away from us and ran toward him, wrapping herself around his legs, holding on for dear life. He hugged her and said, "Jesus loves you." He smiled and patted her, assuming she would go back to her mother. She wouldn't let go. She kept clinging to Him and laughing, looking up into his eyes and calling His name. She wasn't about to let go of her Jesus.

I think God stopped whatever was going on in heaven that day and made all the angels watch Bailey. "Now, look there! That's what I meant when I said, 'Of such is the kingdom of heaven'".

Bailey's reaction should be our reaction every day. When we think of Him: who He is, what He did for us, and what He offers us, how can we do anything less than worship Him in awe?

Author's note: I first wrote this story in 1999 and have shared it with a number of groups over the past years through women's retreats, luncheons, and on Jennifer Rothschild's ministry website, with permission for it to be shared as long as the copyright information was attached. Several amazing things happened as a result of sharing this story. People from all over the world emailed me with their reaction to it, pastors have asked to use it in their Christmas services, and friends received it from friends via email. One family shared that it has become a part of their family's Christmas tradition. Before they share their tree and gifts with one another, the father reads Bailey's Story and they pray. About a year after the story appeared on the website, I received an email from a friend who forwarded it to me with the message: "I thought you might enjoy this story, since you also have a granddaughter named Bailey. As I read it I realized someone had copied the story and removed my name from it before sharing it. I emailed my friend back telling her that I did indeed enjoy the story! The most amusing incident occurred when a woman approached me immediately after I had spoken at women's event in her church. She said she was very disappointed that I told stories that were not true. I asked her to explain, assuring her that every story I had shared in my message was indeed true and written by me personally. She explained that she knew this story wasn't true and wasn't mine because she had received Bailey's Story from a friend in an email. I'm not sure that she ever believed me; I hope she did. It was a special moment in time when God revealed to me the sacrifice He made for you and me because He loves us so much. I was blessed to be there and to have experienced it and to share it. I am honored that others have been touched by reading it.

Thinking About It

? Your Thoughts:

1. What causes us to take our focus off the real meaning of Christmas and Easter?

2. Which part of the story of Jesus did you think of in a new way after reading this chapter?

 Go Deeper

Read through one of the gospels (Matthew, Mark, Luke, John) as if you didn't know how the story ends. Look for fresh meaning through the faith eyes of a child.

Select five verses to commit to memory.

† So What?

What do you want to remember from the story? What difference does this make to you? What will you do?

_____

_____

_____

📖 Study Session

Write your thoughts about God's love and sacrifice after reading the following:

John 3:1-21

Romans 5:6-11

Galatians 4:4

Ephesians 5:2

Hebrews 13:12

I Peter 2:24

I Peter 3:18

I John 1:7

❧ Praying (from 2 Timothy 1:7-8; Romans 1:16)
Lord, thank you that you have not given us a spirit of fear, but of power and love and discipline. I am not ashamed of the Gospel.

_____

_____

_____

_____

Chapter 3

A Picture of The Father

Let them praise His name with dancing!
Let them sing praises to him.
For the Lord takes pleasure in His people.
Psalm 149:3-4

How do you picture God? The example He gave us to understand Him by is fatherhood. A father is to be the picture of God for us. He is to be the example and model of our Heavenly Father. By looking at our fathers, we should be able to see God. No earthly father can be perfect; only our heavenly Father is perfect and can love us perfectly, but there is a pattern given, examples to follow for fathers.

So what kind of picture of God do you have because of your earthly father? Is your picture of God one of an angry, bitter, harsh father, waiting for you to mess up so he can smack you down? Is he all discipline and don'ts? If that's the picture you have of God, I'm sorry; and I want you to know that

that's not God. God is loving and merciful and full of compassion. Psalm 36:7 says, "How priceless is your unfailing love! Both high and low among men find refuge in the shadow of your wings." "The Lord, The Lord, the compassionate and gracious God, slow to anger, abounding in love and faithfulness." Exodus 34

:6 (NIV)

Maybe you picture God as weak and pitiful like today's TV dads, stupid and sorry examples to their wives and children. That's not God. Or, maybe you see a Santa Claus kind of God: Do whatever you want and you still get the presents. Maybe your dad was too busy for you, didn't have or take the time for you and so your picture of God is of one who is aloof and detached, too busy with the war in Iraq and starving children in Zimbabwe to care about you. That's not God. Your God has the hairs of your head numbered and cares for your every thought and need. "Where can I go from your Spirit? Where can I flee from your presence? If I go up to the heavens, you are there. If I rise on the wings of the dawn, if I settle on the far side of the sea, even there your hand will guide me, your right hand will hold me fast…how precious to me are your thoughts." Psalm 139:7-9, 17 (NIV)

I am so fortunate to have known and to have been loved by my grandfathers and my father. It has made seeing God as my heavenly Father so easy to understand. Though not perfect by any stretch, they modeled the unconditional love of a strong and tender father.

I loved my Grandpa Jake, and he loved me. We just called him Jake; for years I thought all grandfathers were either called Pappaw (my mother's father) or Jake (my dad's father). I had the good fortune to be Jake's first granddaughter after six boys, and he thought I was something special. He was, as a father and grandfather, pretty stern with the boys; but the girls…well now, that was a different story. With the girls he had a real soft spot, whether it was his daughters, daughters-in-law, or his granddaughters.

I have so many wonderful memories of him from my earliest childhood to young adulthood when he died a slow and painful death suffocating from emphysema. He was a hard worker, a laborer, who gave away more than he ever made. He was quiet and strong. He was a man's man and a defender of women and children. He was a storyteller and a master on the fiddle. As a child I spent hours standing behind him in his chair combing and fixing his hair with clips and bows. Thinking of it now, I can almost smell his hair tonic. I remember standing on a stool rinsing dishes as he washed them, so my grandmother could go shopping. I remember eating cherry tomatoes as I helped him harvest his garden; he teased me not to eat up his whole crop. I ate more than I could hold because I didn't want him to stop teasing and laughing. It was the best stomachache ever!

He was also my protector on occasion. My mother tells of an incident when I was about two during a family gathering at my grandparents' small home. My mother had scolded me and as she turned away, I kicked her from behind, pealing the skin up the back of her ankle with my heavy, hard-soled walking shoes. She took me aside and spanked me. When she came limping back into the room of adults, Jake was obviously not happy with his favorite daughter-in-law. She explained what I had done. He said, "Well, I don't care. You can spank her at your own house, but not at mine!" Now he would have beaten one of his boys senseless for such a crime, but I was his girl.

My grandparents belonged to a small country church that met in a tiny little chapel with old wooden pews. It must have been Easter or some other special occasion because we were all there visiting and all dressed up. I was maybe three or four and had on a fluffy, ruffley dress stuffed with petticoats and lacy underpants. Grandpa Jake must have been assigned or, more probably, volunteered to take charge of me during this long church service. Now, this was in the days where there were no such things as coloring books or children's activity sets for church. We were to be still and quiet and to obey. I began to squirm. Jake told me to be still. The squirming increased to wriggling and the wriggling to scooting. Jake said, "Be still or you'll get a splinter." I stopped for a while, and then commenced to wriggle around. Then, sure enough! Just as he'd said, my wriggling and squirming landed a big splinter from that old church pew right in my behind. I began to cry, and outside we went. Jake scolded, "I told you to be still or you'd get a splinter. Now look what happened…didn't I tell you?"

Then the operation began: me on the hood of a car, shiny hiney exposed, having a splinter surgically removed by Jake and his pocketknife.

After all was repaired, he said, "Now do you think you can be still?" Back into the church we went, where I sat in his lap and fell asleep. In recalling this story to my parents and other relatives, I said that Jake took me outside and spanked me, to which they all laughed and said, "Absolutely not! He wouldn't have touched you to harm you…even when you deserved it."

I remember on so many occasions when, after a huge meal and playing with cousins, the gathering would begin. It was a time of storytelling and music, and it centered around Jake. Stories were told over and over and over and over. Jake would take out his fiddle and play. We little ones would dance and twirl to his music until we tired out or our parents tired of us. We would then sit up next to a parent or favorite aunt or uncle and drift off to sleep. I'm not sure there's a better, safer feeling than falling to sleep in the presence of those you love, knowing that you are safe. And then being slightly roused by your father as his picks you up and says, "Shhh...we're going home now. Oh, what a picture of our heavenly Father. In His family we have such peace knowing that in His arms we are safe, and that He will carry us home.

I only have faded memories of those early years, but I clearly know how true my grandfather's love and compassion for me and all his grandchildren were because I was given the precious gift of watching him treat my little daughter the same way. When I would visit them, even though his hair was grayer and thinner and he could barely breathe, he wanted his first great-granddaughter nearby. She would dance and twirl and tumble for him as he sat in his chair with his oxygen tank nearby. "Watch me! Jake, watch me!" If she would get too rambunctious in her performances for him, I would get on to her to settle down, afraid she would make him sicker. He would say, "You leave her alone; she's not bothering me. You go tend to whatever you were doing." My, how quickly they turn on you! I thank God I was allowed to see him with her; it was a replay and confirmation of his love for me as a child.

My grandfather stayed in the hospital for weeks and weeks slowly dying. He never complained; he never blamed. On one of my dad's daily visits, he tucked my daughter under his coat and sneaked her up to see Grandpa Jake before he died. Since I lived in another town, I didn't get to go see him very often. How I wish I had gone every day. There are so many things I wish I had said to him that cannot be said now. How I wonder about what he thought about certain things. How I wonder if I ever said, "I love you so much. You made a difference in my life." Why do we wait for the funeral to share the love in our hearts?

Jake loved children and he left his legacy of grandfathering to my dad, who has been ridden, bitten, combed, kicked, wet on, and thrown up on time after time by his grandchildren and now great grandchildren. I don't know of any man who is a better grandfather, anywhere, ever. He lives out Jesus' words, "Permit the children to come to me and do not hinder them; for the kingdom of God belongs to such as these." Mark 10:14

> *Behold, children are a gift of the Lord; the fruit of the womb is a reward.*
> *Like arrows in the hand of a warrior, so are the children of one's youth.*
> *How blessed is the man whose quiver is full of them…*
> Psalm 127:3-5

How then is a father to show us God in today's world? The Bible teaching is clear. Lead, Live, and Love.

1. **A father is to lead**—A father is to be the spiritual leader of his home. We hear that all the time. What does it mean? It doesn't mean he is a slave driver or demeaning boss. He is the servant leader. Just as God commanded the men of Israel to be and to teach their children, so are our fathers today. Deuteronomy 6:1-25 offers the same pertinent challenge to fathers today as it did thousands of years ago. When a father leaves the spiritual aspects of raising his children to the mother or to the church, he is disobeying God and missing an immeasurable blessing. Look carefully at the directions in verses 5-9 and 20-21.

➤ Verse 5 commands us to love the Lord with all of our heart soul, mind and strength. Jesus quoted this in the New Testament when he was asked about the most important commandment.

➤ Verse 6 commands that His Word should be on our heart. We have to know the Word to live it and teach it. It has to be personal, not about rules and relations, but about a relationship.

➤ Verse 7 commands fathers to teach God's Word to your children (impress them on your children). When is that possible in today's busy world? It happens in many ways, both purposeful and incidental. We are to talk about them when you sit in your house, walk by the way, lie down, rise up. Isn't that all the time?

➢ Verse 8 sounds strange to us today. Perhaps our application of this command can be thought of this way. We are to bind them on our <u>hands</u> (in all you do, your work) on our <u>foreheads</u> (in all your thoughts, your mind).

➢ Verse 9 requires that we write them on our doorposts. Not literally, but all should see what your home stands for. What does our home say about us? Can we say what Joshua said in Joshua 24:15, "As for me and my house, we will serve the Lord?"

These are truly difficult times for families just as it was for the children of Israel. They were heading into a land full of evil. Who do you want leading your family? If you don't lead and teach your children, someone else will be glad to—the media, their friends, or other families who don't share your faith.

Fathers, when you lead, your children can see God through you; a picture that will never be forgotten.

2. **A father is to live it**—A father is to live out his faith in front of his family as a model and to leave a legacy of faith. It should be like the disciples saying to Jesus, "Show us the Father." And Jesus saying, "He who has seen me, has seen the Father." John 14:8

➢ Deuteronomy 6:10-12 reminded the children of Israel that they are about to inherit a land for which they did not work and did not deserve, but that God had provided. The message to us is to never forget that everything belongs to God. It is by his grace that we have what we have and are what we are. We are to live grateful lives.

➢ Verses 13-19 reminded them to keep the commands so that it would "go well". Always doing right and living in the integrity of the Lord speaks volumes.

➢ Verse 20 and 21 may be the most important. When our children ask us why, we should be ready with the answer. Can you share with your children what God has done in your life? Can you say with the man healed of his blindness, "I don't understand it all, but this I know…I once was blind and now I see!" (from John 9:25)

At a funeral I recently attended, I listened as a young man gave the eulogy for his grandfather. Through tears, he expressed how thankful he was to find out in the last days of his grandfather's life that he had a relationship with the Lord. I was also thankful to hear that, but thought how sad it was for that young man and his entire family that he had spent a lifetime wondering about such a thing. God has called men and all of us to live our faith and to leave a legacy of faith to our children. Children don't have to agree or even like it, but they should at least know what we believe and why and should see that we walk the talk. No matter what else we leave our children, they should have no doubt about our relationship with the Lord. Some people say that faith is a private matter; I see no validation for that anywhere in the Bible—Old or New Testament. What I do see over and over again are the commands to live our faith out loud. There are no secret-agent Christians. As fathers and as mothers we are to live out the fruit of the Spirit—love, joy, peace, patience, kindness, goodness, faithfulness, gentleness, and self-control.

Your children will learn how to treat their children by how you treated them. Men, your daughters will either feel good or bad about themselves as women by how you treat them and how they see you treat women. Your sons are learning how to treat their wives by how you treat your wife. When you love your wife as Christ loved the church, you're modeling for your children the kind of God we have.

Fathers, when you live out your faith in front of your children, they can see God through you.

3. **A Father is to Love** his children as God loves His. Fatherly love is a combination of affection and discipline. Edwin Cole in *Maximized Manhood* says that Jesus is the perfect combination of tough and tender, and that manhood and Christianity should be synonymous.

Ephesians 6:4 says, "Fathers, do not provoke your children to anger; but bring them up in the discipline and instruction of the Lord."

> *How great is the love the Father has lavished on us, that we should be called the children of God! And that is what we are!* I John 3:1 (NIV)

Deuteronomy 7:6-9 reminds us whose we are! We are God's; we belong to Him; He has chosen us. Not because we're so great...but because He is!

In his book, *The Cross and the Switchblade*, Nicky Cruz described how hard it was to witness to the young men in gangs on the streets of New York City. He said he couldn't use the biblical example of God the Father at first because these men had such a poor view of fathers. They could not get past that image to understand God. Those who work in the prison ministry say that many of the incarcerated are basically the fatherless—they either didn't have a father or the one they had was so bad it was part of what led them to where they are today—in prison, repeating the cycle with their own families.

You may feel like the fatherless also. Father's Day may be a painful day for you. Maybe you don't have a father or the one you have is anything but the picture of God. The Bible speaks to that. God speaks very strongly about two groups of people—the widow and the fatherless. He says that He is *a father to the fatherless and a judge for the widows, is God in His holy habitation. God makes a home for the lonely*..." Psalm 68:5-6

The church has the essential role here, as well. One version says, *God puts the lonely in families*. The Children's Bible states, *God gives lonely people a family*. That's us: the body; the church, Christians. We are to be the family for the fatherless and the lonely. We are to comfort others as He did us. *And He is the God of all comfort!* (2 Corinthians 1:3) Psalm 34:18 reassures us that, *The Lord is near to the brokenhearted, and saves those who are crushed in spirit.*

When God has become your father, He redeems and heals. Paul said,

> *For all who are led by the Spirit of God, these are the sons of God. For you have not received a spirit of slavery leading to fear again,*

but you have received a spirit of adoption as sons by which we cry out, "Abba! Father!" The Spirit Himself bears witness with our spirit that we are children of God, and if children, heirs also, heirs of God and fellow-heirs with Christ...
Romans 8:14-17

You may also find yourself in the situation of being a stepfather to someone else's children, or you have a stepfather, or your children are in the care of a stepfather. Well, guess what? So did Jesus! What a man Joseph must have been! We know so little about Joseph and yet what we do know gives us a powerful example to follow. He loved God. He listened to God. He was a man of integrity. He loved the child's mother. He loved the child as his own. He had the highest calling any man could have—to raise the Son of God. To raise a child for God! That's what all stepfathers and stepmothers are called to do. Not to raise a child for the biological father, but for God. Wow! What a privilege. How thankful I am on this day for the man who answered the call, the Joseph Call, to raise my two children for God. How faithful and committed he has been. And, now the time, love, and discipline he spent is joyfully returned to him in honor and respect from the children he committed to raise for the Lord.

Jesus had some strong words about how people should treat children and the weak. Jesus said,

Whoever then humbles himself as this child, he is the greatest is the kingdom of heaven. And whoever receives one such child in my name receives me; but whoever causes one of these little ones who believe in Me

to stumble, it is better for him that a heavy millstone be hung around his neck, and that he be drowned in the depths of the sea. Matthew 18:4-6

Fathers, when you love your children, they can see the love of God through you.

You may be thinking that it's too late, that you've missed your opportunity.

Please understand that with God, it is never too late as long as we have a breath. He is the God of second chances and third chances and so on. Perhaps Jesus sketched the best picture of God the Father when He told the story of a loving, waiting father in Luke 15. A father with two sons—one who stayed in devotion, faithfully working; one who left in rebellion, destroying everything he had and breaking his fathers' heart. He loved the son who was steadfast, and longed for the son who was lost. When the wayward son came to his senses and headed home, the father came running. It didn't matter what the son had done or where he had been. It only mattered that he was home. That's the picture of our heavenly Father: it doesn't matter where you've been or what you've done, He just wants you to come home. He loves you.

Author's Note: This teaching was originally given in 2002 as a sermon on Father's Day and then written as a Father's Day gift to my Father, subtitled, *A Tribute to My Father and His Father.*

Thinking About It

? Your Thoughts:

1. Who is an earthly model of a father for you?
2. In what ways did or do you see your earthly father raising you for God?
3. To whom can you be a representation of God?

Go Deeper

Read Proverbs focusing on instructions for families.

Select five verses to commit to memory.

† So What?

What do you want to remember from the story? What difference does this make to you? What will you do?

_____

_____

_____

📖 Study Session

Write your thoughts about God's love as our heavenly Father after reading the following:

Exodus 34:6

2 Chronicles 20:21

Psalm 27:10

Psalm 36:5-7

Psalm 89:26

Psalm 103:10-17

Psalm 139:7-10

Proverbs 17:6

Isaiah 64:8

Jeremiah 23:23-24

Matthew 6:1-34

2 Corinthians 8:6

1 John 3:1

☙ **Praying** (from Psalm 68:5-6; 2 Corinthians 1:3)

Lord, thank you that you are a Father to the fatherless and make a home for the lonely. Thank you for being the God of all comfort.

_____

_____

_____

_____

Chapter 4

Granny's Grace

...My grace is sufficient for you, for power is perfected in weakness.
2 Corinthians 12:9

Mercy, Grace, Saved. Redeemed.

There are so many powerful words that we use interchangeably and even loosely. Mercy me! Good gracious! Merciful heavens! If we really think about what these words mean in the context of who God is, we might be more thoughtful.

Consider this:

Have you ever been accused of something you didn't do? So was Jesus.

Have you ever had to pay for something someone else did? So did Jesus.

Have you ever had to give up something you deserve to someone else who didn't deserve it? So did Jesus.

Have you ever forgiven someone a debt they owed you and never mentioned it again? Jesus did.

Have you ever loved someone who didn't know how to love you back so much that you offered them everything to show your love? God did.

Have you ever sacrificed by giving a gift and then it was not received or appreciated? Jesus did, too.

Would you give your child to be sacrificed so that those who treated you badly could live? Our Heavenly Father did.

Would you then offer to adopt into your own family those who accepted your sacrificial gift? He does.

That's is a picture of *grace* and *mercy*. It is a picture of God. He is loving, merciful, and gracious. It means: full of love—unconditional love, full of mercy, and full of grace. To really grasp what He has done for us and wants us to do for others, we have to understand both grace and mercy as two distinct qualities. And, before we can give grace to others, we must understand what it is and say yes to grace in our own lives. Such was the case in my grandmother's life.

The year was 1946; it was September. The world was recovering from World War II and a depression and my grandmother was six months pregnant with her ninth child. My dad, the fifth child in a hard-working family, was fourteen. It was on September 14, that my grandmother and grandfather received the news that their 6-year-old daughter had been killed in a car-train accident. She was in a car with her older married sister, brother-in-law and an aunt. They were stopped at a crossing waiting for a train that was approaching. An approaching vehicle didn't see the crossing or the stopped car. The speeding vehicle hit them from behind pushing their car onto the tracks. The husband and wife got out before the train arrived, but not the little girl or the aunt. The aunt was severely injured, but survived. The little girl did not. The news devastated my grandparents and their other children. My grandfather would later say that he never really was the same after that. Making a bad situation worse, was the news that the driver of the car who hit them had been drinking. He was not intoxicated, but had had a couple of drinks to celebrate his acceptance to medical school. He and his fiancé had been celebrating, and he was rushing to get her to her job as a nurse at the hospital. The state filed criminal charges against him for manslaughter, and the ensuing trial proved to be a strain on everyone involved.

My grandmother was a woman of faith. She loved God with all her heart and spent time in the Word every day. As the difficult trial progressed, my grandmother and other relatives sat and listened to the proceedings day after day. Near the end of the trial, as a conviction seemed apparent, my grandmother asked to take the stand. Everyone thought she would talk about how her life had been ruined and that someone needed to pay for the life that was taken. But, instead, she testified on the young man's behalf. She said that she knew it was an accident, that she had sons who might have done the very same thing. She held absolutely no hard feelings toward him. Nothing could bring her child back, and she saw no reason to take another life in retribution. She had forgiven him as God had forgiven all, and she wanted him to be able to have the life that God had planned for him: to become a doctor and save lives. Largely because of my grandmother's testimony, he was acquitted and went on to become a doctor. Even though his carelessness had taken the life of her child, she wanted him to have a good life. She did not want him to be punished. He never ceased to show his gratitude for her mercy. My grandmother received Christmas cards and letters every year until her death some forty years later.

Think of it. It is a picture of what Jesus did for us. There was the crime, the death of the innocent; the verdict was guilty without the witness who intervened, and the life of freedom. My grandmother lay herself, her feelings, her hurts on the altar for a stranger whose carelessness killed her child. She sacrificed hate and bitterness in love. That's MERCY! But that's not all. She could have just gone to him privately and said, "I forgive you," and let the trial continue. But, she publicly testified on his behalf. She gave him a gift. She did him a favor. She stood in the gap between the guilty and the judge, pleading for mercy. And the guilty was proclaimed innocent. He got what her child deserved: life and freedom. She did him a favor; that's GRACE.

Here's the difference:

➤   Mercy means not punishing a guilty person that you have the right to punish.

➤   Grace is offering an undeserved gift or favor.

That's what God did for us. Because He is full of mercy, he forgives our sins and declares us not guilty. But it gets better! Grace is better! He not only declares us not guilty, but then He offers us life—abundant life! He gives us a gift. If we, in faith, accept His grace, we are not only set free from our slavery to sin, but we are adopted into His family as children—joint heirs with Christ. Someone once succinctly put it this way: GRACE= <u>God's Riches At Christ's Expense</u>. GRACE!

It's not just God saying, "Okay, I forgive you; good luck; have a nice life." That would be merciful. But it's as if He says, "You are forgiven; you are not guilty. Now come sit at my banquet table; sit in my son's place and enjoy everything that is mine!" Wow! That's Grace.

Have you ever played monopoly? This isn't a perfect example, but maybe it will make the point. Let's say I am a child and am going to play a game of monopoly with my family. Now, my father bought the game; it is his. We are in his house; he paid for it. I am his child; everything I have He brought for me. As the game progresses, I, being childish and foolish, have squandered my allowance and only have Baltic Avenue and a little money left to show for it. Daddy owns Boardwalk and Park Place, in addition to many other properties, and all have three hotels. As I travel around the board, I luckily miss some high dollar rental properties until I come to Boardwalk. I land right on it. Well, there's no way I can pay. Even if I gave all my money and all my property, it would still not be enough. I cry out to my Daddy, who owns it all and who loves me. If he is merciful; he says, "It's okay. You don't have to pay this time. I won't count it against you. You can pass for free." He cancels my debt. That's mercy—not counting something against me. What kindness. But what if He said, "Not only am I not going to charge you the rent due to me; but because I love you so much, I'm going to give you Boardwalk and Park Place with all the hotels. They are yours. It will cost you nothing. All you have to do is accept them because you love me. And not only that, but every time you land on other high rent property, I'll go with you and pay it too." That is grace; bestowing on me a gift that I don't deserve and can't pay for. I just have to receive it and love the giver.

Would I ever be so foolish to say, "No, thanks. I'm really not interested. I'll just go out." Or, would I ever just say, " Thanks for the mercy. I accept the free pass, but I pay my own way. I don't take charity. How about an installment plan? I'll give you $100 every time I pass GO." No one would do that! But that's exactly what we do when we don't recognize and receive God's gift to us—His grace.

Amazing Grace! how sweet the sound… Who hasn't heard the words of that beautiful hymn? You might think that some pious, godly preacher-type man wrote those words. But there is an amazing story of grace behind the writing of *Amazing Grace*. We would be hard pressed to imagine anyone more sinful and blasphemous than John Newton, born in 1725. When, as a child of seven, his mother died, Newton went to sea with his father, a captain of a merchant ship. His mother had been a godly woman who taught him to read by age three and instilled in his memory scriptures, hymns and poems. At sea, John began a decline into rebellion and sin that lasted until he was twenty-four. He was on one occasion a slave trader in North Africa. He was so wicked that even his crews considered him little more than an animal. A harrowing experience during weeks at sea was used by the Lord to change him. Near starvation and shipwreck, Newton began a sincere effort to become right with God. On a small island off the coast of North Africa, weak and ill, he gave his life completely to God. The following fourteen years he studied for the ministry and at age thirty-nine became a pastor in England. He later published a hymnal in which he placed 281 of his own works, including *Amazing Grace*. In his later years, with eyesight and memory failing, it became necessary for him to have an assistant aid him in the pulpit. One Sunday, Newton repeatedly read the words, "Jesus Christ is so precious."

"You've already said that twice," whispered his assistant, "Go on."

"I said it twice and I'll say it again," he shouted, "Jesus Christ is precious!" Newton died in 1807 at eight-two years of age and had this epitaph etched on a plain marble slab:

John Newton, clerk, once an infidel and libertine, a servant of slaves in Africa, was by the rich mercy of our Lord and Savior, Jesus Christ preserved, restored, pardoned, and appointed to preach the faith he had long labored to destroy.

Thinking About It

? Your Thoughts

1. How do you recognize grace, unmerited favor from God, in your own life?

2. When did you receive God's gift of grace by saying yes to Christ?

3. How are you growing in grace? How are you becoming more like Jesus?

4. Does grace flow through you? What grace acts are you going to extend to others?

📖 Study Session

Read the following study sections and Bible passages to understand the attributes of God's grace and mercy.

1. **You have to <u>recognize</u> grace.** Do you see the difference in mercy and grace? Can you describe the difference in your own words?

   _____

   _____

2. **You have to <u>receive</u> it**. It is a gift. Read Ephesians 2:8-9.

   ▪ *For by grace you have been saved through faith; and not of yourselves, it is the gift of God not as a result of works, that no one should boast.*

   ▪ Listen to Ephesians 2:8-10 in the New Living Translation: *God saved you by his special favor when you believed. And you can't take credit for this; it is a gift from God. Salvation is not a reward for the good things we have done, so none of us can boast about it. For we are God's masterpiece, He created us anew in Christ Jesus, so that we can do the good things he planned for us long ago.*

Go back and underline the words that describe grace.

☑ **It is from God**.

John 3:16: *For God love the world in such a way that He gave his one and only son, that whoever believes in Him should not perish, but have eternal life.*

☑ **It is a covenant**. It is a promise we can count on. He established the covenant and He keeps it.

Because of what Jesus did, I have direct access to God; I don't have to go through anyone else, I don't have to be good enough and hope that someday I might make it. Jesus was beaten and died and rose again so that I have the rights as a child of the King! Hebrews 4:16 tells us to draw near to the throne of grace and receive mercy and find grace. *So let's walk right up to Him and get what He is so ready to give. Take the mercy, accept the help.* (*The Message*)

☑ **It takes humility**. Read Titus 3:3-7

Just as in my Monopoly game, where I couldn't pay the debt even if I wanted to, we can't earn God's grace, pay for it, be good enough for it, or deserve it. We have to accept it. Think how God feels when we try to receive it in any other way than how it is offered, "Let me pay you for that." Or, when we deny it? "No, thanks."

☑ **It takes faith**. That's our only part.

I don't have to understand it all to receive it. John 1:12-13 -- *But as many as received Him He gave the right to become the children of God, even those who believed in His name.*

Romans 10:9 -- *If you <u>confess</u> with your mouth "Jesus as Lord" and <u>believe</u> in your heart that God raised Him from the dead, you <u>shall</u> be saved.*

☑ **It takes commitment**. Once we say *Yes* to God's gift of grace, we begin a new life. 2 Corinthians 5:17 -- *If any man is in Christ, he is a new creation.*

3. I have to **<u>grow</u>** in it. When I first commit to Christ, whether I am seven years old or seventy-seven years old, I am a babe in Christ. Just as a newborn baby needs to be nourished to grow, so do we as believers. Think of what happens to a newborn that doesn't receive nourishment and comfort. That's what happens to us spiritually. How many people have you seen who have made a commitment and then over time slowly drift away? The desire of all parents' heart when they have a child is for him to grow healthy and strong into all that he can be; that is our heavenly Father's desire for us and He has provided all we need: His Word, His Holy Spirit, His Church.

Then we will no longer be like children, forever changing our minds about what we believe because someone has told us something different or because someone has cleverly lied to us and made the lie sound like the truth. Instead, we will hold to the truth in love, becoming more and more in every way like Christ, who is the head of his body, the church. Ephesians 4:14-15 NLT

4. I have to **extend** it to others.

- Grace is to flow through me. What if in my game of Monopoly, I took the gracious gift and then set out to win my own way at all costs? I want all the money, all the property. My daddy lands on Park Place (which he gave to me) and I say, "Pay up Buddy! You owe me!" My brothers and sisters land on other property I won and ask for mercy. "Sorry! Too bad...pay up! That's life!" Here's what breaks God's heart: When I don't give the love, mercy and grace to others that He so richly gives to me. Remember Jesus' example when Peter asked how many times he should forgive a brother who had wronged him? Peter thought he was really being generous saying seven times. The religious law at the time only required three. Jesus' answer of seventy times seven really means, "every time." (Matthew 18:21-33) When asked how we were to live as Christ's followers, Jesus said it was all summed up in these words from Matthew 22:37-40:

You shall love the Lord your God with all your heart, and with all your soul, and with all your mind. This is the greatest and foremost commandment. The second is like it; you shall love your neighbor as yourself. On these two commandments depend the whole Law and the Prophets.

Go Deeper

1.   Read Romans chapter 8 and Paul's short letters to the Galatians, Ephesians, Philippians, and Colossians focusing on references to grace and mercy. Select five verses to commit to memory.

2. Write your thoughts about receiving and growing in God's grace after reading the following:

John 3:14-18

Acts 4:12

Romans 3:23-24

Romans 5:8-9

Romans 8:1

2 Corinthians 12:9

Galatians 2:19-21

Ephesians 2:8-10

Ephesians 6:10-20

Colossians 2:6-14

2 Timothy 1:7-14

2 Timothy 2:1

Titus 3:3-7

I Peter 1:13-15; 2:1-3

II Peter 3:18

I John 1:5-10

✝ So What?

What do you want to remember from the story? What difference does this make to you? What will you do?

_____

_____

_____

🕊 Praying (from Titus 3:3-7)

Thank you, Father, that you don't count me righteous on the basis of what I have done, but because of what Jesus did.

_____

_____

_____

_____

P.

K

G(

High

Mowing

But when the Holy Spir
fruit in us: love, joy, peac
gent

ountains

FM 2191

whence shall my help come?
ade heaven and earth.
keeps you will not slumber,
er slumber nor sleep.
shade on your right hand.
r the moon by night.
He will keep your soul.
and your coming In,
er Psalm 121

es with my parents, brothers,
our family car. You know the
other states?" or "Who can
I now know having us play
ling with four wild kids. We
Disneyland or the Grand

Canyon. We took vacations to visit our relatives. I'm so glad. I'm so grateful that we didn't have the money to go to places that can only provide memories of things instead of people. I have a priceless treasure chest of memories I would never trade of summers and Easters and Christmases and Thanksgivings and Fourth of July parades with my grandparents, cousins, aunts and uncles.

One of our favorite places was my parents' hometown. This "downhill-all-the-way" hometown had a Pepto-Bismol pink drive-in movie theater and a grain elevator that was painted bright green. From one of our childhood misspeakings, we all called it the "green alligator". For years I thought all grain elevators were called "alligators". Even now I often have to stop and think of the right word. When traveling to see our grandparents, we had a contest to see who could be the first to spot the green alligator and the pink show. This sighting meant we were only minutes away from Mammaw and Pappaw's house and the wonderful time we always had there! I still feel a little adrenaline rush whenever I travel that highway and come up over the rise that allows me to see the green alligator. It is a traveler's landmark; it is a precious landmark in my life.

Today as I travel these Panhandle Plains, I love to look at the dramatic scenery. I often try to imagine what it was like for the explorers and settlers who saw these places for the first time. Flat grassy land as far as you can see and then the surprise of the majestic canyon slashes through the landscape for hundreds of miles. Stark features, vast horizons, brilliant colors. Sunsets, oh the sunsets! Only for a moment can you capture the brilliant oranges and purples reflected from the dust and clouds of these flatlands. But, oh that moment! Everything stands out against the vastness and nothingness – windmills, a lone tree, and cattle having what I imagine to be an afternoon coffee or soda break at their local watering hole catching up on the latest bovine business. Then, there are the looming, solitary giants of the sprawling fields.

Grain elevators. Huge concrete towers. Peaks of gray. High plains mountains. Standing alone, they break the flatness. It may sound funny, but I love these grain elevators. I am sometimes awed and cowed by their vastness, unaccustomed to the height and breadth of these peaks of the plains casting long shadows and creating strong crosswinds.

I recently experienced some life lessons in elevators. Since I often travel to the same towns, I sometimes try out new routes to break the boredom of the busy interstate highways. Coming home from a day of leading teachers in a small town about fifty miles from home, I discovered a route that enabled me to not only save time, but also to avoid construction and heavy traffic on the highway. It was a beautiful day and nothing pressing was waiting for me, so I embarked on a traveling adventure. All I had to do was take the highway south to the next small town, then west a few miles to the grain elevator on the right. Then, a turn left on the Farm-to-Market road would lead me to the Interstate and easy access home. It worked out great.

see what you can really glean from this!" What was the spiritual learning? God began to reveal powerful spiritual lessons to me. Jesus is my landmark, my elevator, the only way to the Father. The route I choose to follow is His will for my life, my journey as a Christian.

Lesson # 1

How much easier it would have been from the beginning if I'd used my map and followed the direction to the road I needed. Follow the map. Study His word. God provides instructions. The Holy Spirit will reveal His will for my life through His word and through prayer.

Thy Word is a lamp unto my feet and a light unto my path.

Psalm 119-105

Lesson #2

To get to the landmark, the elevator, I had to keep my eyes on the landmark and only one road led to it. Keep my eyes on Jesus, my landmark! Line up everything with Him. All other roads lead to nowhere. They are bad angles, even if they look good. There is only one way.

I am the Way, and the Truth, and the Life, no one comes to the Father but through me.

John 14:6

Lesson #3

I took some wrong paths thinking they were right. Some routes were clearly wrong; some looked right and were deceptively wrong. My thinking that a path is right, doesn't make it so. My feeling that it is right, doesn't make it so. Just because others exit, doesn't mean I can. Some things are clearly wrong - wrong path, wrong direction - some are more shrewd: they even look right ...for a while. Without the map and the Landmark, I am easily deceived.

There is a way which seems right to a man, but its end is the way of death
Proverbs 14:12

Lesson #4

When I took a wrong exit, the sooner I got back on path, the better. The longer I wait and the farther I go on the wrong path, the harder it is on me and the later I am to arrive at my destination. No matter how many wrong paths I take in life, God still gives me another chance. The longer I wait and the farther I go away from Christ, the harder it is to find my way back; the landmark begins to diminish. The Savior's awesome promise is that even if I stray so far that I cannot even see the landmark; signs can lead me back to Christ; He is still there, waiting, wanting.

The Lord is not slow about His promise, as some count slowness, but is patient toward you, not wishing for anyone to perish, but for all to come to repentance.
2 Peter 3:9

Jesus Christ is the same yesterday and today, yes and forever.

Hebrews 13:8

Lesson #5

The closer I got to the landmark, the larger it got. If I'm on the wrong path, the landmark begins to diminish because I am moving away, not because it isn't there or because it is moving away from me. The landmark doesn't move. The more I know of Jesus, the hungrier I am, and the more I want to know. I want to see Jesus, be with Him, and learn from Him. The closer I am to the Landmark, the larger He is, the louder His Word is, the clearer the Way is.

...But whatever things were gain to me, those things I have counted as loss for the sake of Christ. More than that, I count all things to be loss in view of the surpassing value of knowing Christ Jesus my Lord, for whom I have suffered the loss of all things, and count them but rubbish in order that I may gain Christ, and may be found in Him, not having a righteousness of my own derived from the Law, but that which is through faith in Christ, the righteousness which comes from God on the basis of faith, that I may know Him, and the power of His resurrection, and the fellowship of His sufferings, being conformed to His death...I press on toward the goal for the prize of the upward call of God in Christ Jesus. Philippians 3:7-10, 14

...let us run with endurance the race that is set before us, fixing our eyes on Jesus, the author and perfecter of faith. Hebrews 12:1-2

God blessed me so much with this teaching. I reflected on it often, especially as I traveled this road. Every time I pass any elevator, I am impressed with its singular presence. David used the language of his day from his culture to express his love and devotion for God from the Psalms: *The Lord is my Rock and my shelter; The Lord is my shepherd...*

If David were here today and were a high plains shepherd maybe he would say with me as he looked up into the vast sky, "The Lord is my elevator, my landmark, an ever present help."

I thought this was the end of the lesson. But I had more to learn, much more.

Have you noticed anything missing from my story? Any tiny little, yet important, detail you've wondered about? Well...see if it becomes apparent as I describe other lessons I learned when God enrolled me in High Plains Elevators-Advanced Course.

Twice, I took this new route enjoying my newly acquired thoughts and lessons. How beautiful was the playa lake at the curve in the road, filled with rainwater from a series of autumn thunderstorms, alive with geese landing and taking off after dining in the surrounding wheat fields. I was also distracted with writing a little poem about cows at their "bovine soda shop"—quite taken with that image.

On the third or fourth trip, having left well before sunrise, I realized I had a big problem as I pulled onto the interstate and as dawn crested: FOG! Not just a light mist, but thick, pea soup fog. You may be wondering why limited visibility was such a problem. It has to do with that little detail about this route that I should have known but had not worried about because it was insignificant on a clear day, but oh so critical under foggy conditions. Any guesses? Yes! The road number! I had still never paid attention to the road number. When skies were blue and vision was clear, why worry about details such as road signs? After all when I could clearly see my landmark, numbers were trivial.

But in this fog, I was disoriented. For me, there are few things more frightening than a driver not being able to see beyond the end of the car and yet having to continue moving forward, fearful of meeting someone else coming the other way just as disoriented.

This was worse than the first time I had tried to find the road. I couldn't see my landmark or the exits or even the road at times. I had to guess again: I had to feel my way. I was fearful and lost. I was confused. Was it after the third or the fourth exit? How many miles was it? Should I pull over and wait? What if someone hit me? Seeing the fourth exit, I decided to try it. After crossing the overpass and driving a while, I was still uncertain. Then, I came to the curve in the road. Thank Goodness! That wonderful old curve! It had twice reassured me that I was on the right road. Then, doubt. Did the other roads have curves too? I had never taken those other roads. I only hoped it was my curve on my road. And how long was this road? I still couldn't see my landmark; I had nothing with which to align. I could only see the unstriped road in front of me and the bar ditch to my right. I couldn't see things in front of me, things coming at me, or things behind me. And where were those silly geese? And gossipy cows?

I was almost upon my landmark before I saw it. What joy. What relief. I didn't realize that every muscle in my body was tensed until I relaxed at the sight of that beautiful mountain. What thankfulness…What a dummy! I realized immediately that I was only prepared for this journey under ideal conditions. I had not prepared to travel under adverse conditions. Because I didn't know the road number, my journey was uncertain, stressful, doubtful when conditions were bad.

My new hard-learned lessons?

➢ The way will not always be evident. I will not always see clearly. Storms will rage; tests will come. If I have followed the map, if I am in God's Word, I can travel with confidence, even if I can't see the path clearly. The road number represents His promises to me. His promises are true whether I can see clearly or not. If I had known the road number, I would have known I was on the right road whether it felt like it or not, whether I could see or not. All I have to do is follow and believe, whether I feel like it or not. When the conditions of this world cloud my vision of my landmark, I can trust His promises.

Now faith is the assurance of things hoped for, the conviction of things not seen. Hebrews 12:1

Even though I walk through the valley of the shadow of death, I fear no evil; for Thou art with me. Psalm 23:4

➢ He is so faithful to give us little reassurances along the way, like the curve in the road that said, "Keep going, you're on the right road."

And Lo, I am with you always... Matthew 28:20

➢ I can't let fog keep me where I am. I have to get to my destination. I have to see Jesus! I can't stop just because I can't see the end. I must go in faith. If I'm not prepared with the promises, then the storms and the fog of life can make the trip overwhelming.

These things I have spoken to you that in me you may have peace. In the world you have tribulation, but take courage; I have overcome the world."
John 16:33

➤ The elevator was there. My not being able to see it didn't change that fact. Paul penned it this way,

Who shall separate us from the love of Christ? Shall tribulation, or distress, or persecution, or famine, or nakedness, or peril, or sword?...But in all these things we overwhelmingly conquer through Him who loved us. For I am convinced that neither death, nor life, nor angels, nor principalities, nor things present, nor things to come, nor powers, nor height, nor depth, nor any other created thing, shall be able to separate us from the love of God which is in Christ Jesus our Lord. Romans 8:35-39

The next time you leave on a journey and every time you see a mountain, a forest, or one of our concrete high plains mountains, will you stop and praise God? Will you let it remind you of the Way and the Truth and the Life? And if you too don't have mountains, will you consider these manmade concrete peaks and share the psalmist's cry?

I will lift up my eyes to the mountains;
From whence shall my help come?
My help comes from the Lord,
Who made heaven and earth.
Psalm 121:1-2

Thinking About It

? Your Thoughts:

1. Describe a time when you were lost or afraid. How did you get through it?
2. What feature or structure reminds you of the awesome power of God?
3. What do you need in order to keep your focus during times of stress and uncertainty?

Go Deeper

Read Psalm 23, 46, and 91.

Select five verses to commit to memory.

† So What?

What do you want to remember from the story? What difference does this make to you? What will you do?

_____

_____

_____

📖 Study Session

1. Write your thoughts about receiving and growing in God's grace after reading the following:

    2 Samuel 22:3, 51

    Psalm 18:1-6, 16-18, 30-36, 46-49

    Psalm 59:16-17

    Psalm 61:1-4

    Psalm 71:1-5

    Proverbs 8:17

    Isaiah 30:21

    Jeremiah 29:13

    Amos 5:4

    Habakkuk 2:1

    Matthew 6:33

    2 Corinthians 5:7

    Philippians 3:14

🕊 **Praying** (from Psalm 16:11)

Father God, forgive me when I lose sight of your will and take the wrong paths. Thank you for your guidance and provisions. Thank you for the storms and for the promises. Thank you for landmarks and lessons. Thank you for the life we have through Jesus Christ our Lord and Savior. Thank you for making known to me the path of life.

Chapter 6

Mowing Without the Blade
A Journey to JOY

Those who plant in tears will harvest with shouts of joy.
They weep as they go to plant their seed,
But they sing as they return with the harvest.
Psalm 126:5-6 NLT

Did you grow up thinking your family was like all other families until some event caused you to realize that families were different? I always thought that the way I was brought up was normal until that one day when I realized that my family was not like other families. It was the day someone told me I was weird because I was sometimes taken to or picked up from school in an ambulance or hearse. You see, I grew up in a funeral home family. My dad and his brothers were funeral directors. They owned funeral homes and cemeteries. And, in those days, also ran the ambulance service in our town. Thinking back on it now, the ambulance/funeral home combination seems like a huge conflict of interest!

It was normal. It was <u>our</u> normal. We children used to fight over whose turn it was to spend the night with Daddy when he had to stay at the funeral home with a body. Sounds strange to you? It was our life. It was our normal.

The summer after I graduated from college I moved back home to teach school, and I needed to earn some money. The man who mowed the cemetery for my dad had quit, and he needed someone to mow. Ahaa! It was the perfect solution. I needed money and a tan, so I talked Daddy into letting me mow, even though I had never run a lawn mower before. "Honey, have you ever used a riding mower?"

Slightly offended at the question, I responded, "Well, no, but how hard can it be? I have a college degree!" Assuring him I knew what to do, I prepared myself for the job. All oiled down with tanning lotion, radio headphones on my ears, I started the tractor mower and took off. It was a huge area, taking about 20 minutes to go around the outside. I had almost finished my second sweep around when I saw Daddy waving at me. I waved back. No, he wasn't waving; he was motioning to me to stop and come to him. So I drove over to where he was, and he yelled over the sound of the motor, "What are you doing?"

I yelled back, "I'm mowing!"

"No you're not! You don't have the blade down!" I had been driving around and around and not mowing one inch. "Didn't you notice the grass wasn't shorter behind you?"

"Well, I never checked. I was trying to watch where I was going."

I <u>thought</u> I knew what I was doing. I <u>looked</u> like a mower. I <u>smelled</u> like a mower. I <u>sounded</u> like a mower. I was covered in dirt and dead grass, and smelled of sweat and baby oil. The motor was roaring. But I wasn't mowing; I was really only driving a tractor, stirring up dust, not accomplishing what I was supposed to do, what I was hired to do.

Mowing without the blade down.

Can you relate? Do you ever feel like you are just going through life, making a lot of noise and stirring up stuff, but not really making a difference? Not accomplishing what you set out to do?

Mowing without the blade down was the story of my life until I completely gave it to the Lord. I looked like a Christian. I tried to act like a Christian. I sounded like a Christian. But my life was like mowing without the blade down. I was working extremely hard, never checking to see if I was making a difference, if *the grass was shorter behind me*. I had no JOY.

What about you?

If you look at your life as a journey, what roads and paths have brought you to this place today? Has it been smooth, straight, paved roads? Or has your way been rough, bumpy, and crooked? Maybe a combination of both? When we choose Jesus, we are on the journey that will eventually lead to eternal life with Him, a secure destination. But, how about the trip? What are we doing on the journey? Jesus intended for the journey to be one filled with love, joy, peace, patience, kindness, goodness, faithfulness, gentleness, self-control: the fruit of the Spirit. Then why are so many not experiencing the fullness and abundance that He promised? Why are so many just barely surviving the journey? It may partly be due to some heavy baggage we carry on board. The baggage is two thieves, **Fear and Regret**, and their friends, Shame, Guilt, Doubt, Blame, Anger, Bitterness, Depression, Flesh, Sadness.

Fear of tomorrow stands in the way of enjoying the trip and trusting the Father. It robs us of the peace of Today. Regrets of yesterday keep us looking back over the past and reliving, repenting, regretting. It robs us of the joy of Today. As long as we are shackled by these thieves, we cannot live in the freedom for which we were saved. Then, we are robbed of receiving and giving the love of God. Jesus came to give us abundant life, not just survival skills!

I don't want to just survive. I want to thrive. I want it all. I want Jesus' love, joy, and peace! How do I get it? How do I keep it? How do I live the life He called me to? The focus of the journey has to be Jesus, not the trip itself or the destination. It's all about Jesus and His cross! It is about who He is, what He did for us, what He offers and requires.

I found that there were four aspects on my journey to JOY, all non-negotiable. We can use the word JOY as an acronym to remember them.

1. **Jesus Offers You – Salvation – Freedom from Sin**
2. **Jesus Over Yesterday – Forgiveness – Freedom from your past**
3. **Jesus, Others, You – Service – Free to serve**
4. **Jesus Owns You – Surrender – Free to grow**

<u>J</u>esus <u>O</u>ffers <u>Y</u>ou – Salvation – You can be free.

This is the first truth. It is about a relationship. Happiness is based on happenings; but true joy comes from a relationship with Jesus Christ.

The only way to be free is through Jesus Christ. Jesus told us, "You shall know the truth and the truth shall make you free….If therefore the Son shall make you free, you shall be free indeed." John 8:32,36

"I am the Way, the Truth, and the Life. No one comes to the Father but through me." Christianity is not about religion—rules, lists, do's and don'ts—it is a relationship with Jesus Christ. In order to be free from the sin problem we have, we must first recognize our condition without Him, our need for Him, and commit ourselves to Him. This is the only way to find true joy.

Satan doesn't want you on this journey with Jesus, and you should know he is a liar and thief. He will do everything in his power to keep you from Jesus and then to defeat you in your Christian walk. Satan would love nothing more than to highjack your journey. Here are some of Satan's lies: "Go ahead and believe there is a God, but that's enough…We are all headed for the same place…Take your time, there is no hurry…Go to church, but don't get excited…Jesus was just a man…you've messed up too bad to get in…There's lots of paths to the final destination…we're all going in the same direction…and so on."

It's not knowing <u>about</u> Him, it is knowing Him, belonging to Him, believing who He said He was. The demons believe <u>about</u> Him. James 2:19

To be free I must believe who He is. Jesus Christ, God the Son, Savior. Think about Him! And what He did for us.

The first step to JOY is accepting the freedom that God offers us through His Son. "For God so loved the world that He gave His only Son that whoever believes in Him shall not perish, but have eternal life." John 3:16 (NIV)

Jesus Over Yesterday – Forgiveness –
You can be free from your past

The second truth on the journey to freedom is realizing that Jesus has the power to forgive all your past sins. It's what He does! You cannot be good enough to earn your salvation. And you can never be bad enough to prevent your salvation.

"If therefore the Son shall make you free, you shall be free indeed." John 8:36

"It was for freedom that Christ has set us free; therefore keep standing firm and do not be subject again to a yoke of slavery." Galatians 5:1

Don't believe Satan's lies when he tells you that you are not worthy or that God can't use you, or that you irrevocably messed up this time. Remember, Satan is a liar. He hates you. He wants you to be defeated.

And never forget that God is true. God loves you. God has a plan for victory in your life. He redeems sinners for His perfect purposes…because that's what we all are!

Let's just look at a few of our heroes of the Bible: If you think God can't use you because of your past, read their stories.

Moses was a murderer and led God's people. Jonah was a preacher who didn't like the mission God gave him, so he tried to run away from God. Even after he was vomited up by the fish and went on to complete his mission, he still had a bad attitude, even after his preaching saved an entire nation. David, called a man after God's own heart, wrote most of the Psalms and was a mighty warrior and king; he was also an adulterer, murderer, and liar to cover his sin. God completely restored him when he repented. Peter denied that he even knew Jesus and ran away scared. Then, he preached one of the greatest sermons ever delivered on Pentecost and 3000 people were saved. And the list goes on. Paul was a religious zealot intent on killing all followers of Jesus until he met the Master himself on the road to Damascus. Paul became the great missionary, writer, and martyr. He summed it up this way:

For we also once were foolish ourselves, disobedient, deceived, enslaved to various lusts and pleasures, spending our life in malice and envy, hateful, hating one another. But when the kindness of God our Savior and His love for mankind appeared, He saved us, not on the basis of deeds which we have done in righteousness, but according to His mercy, by the washing of regeneration and renewing by the Holy Spirit, whom He poured out on us richly through Jesus Christ our Savior, that being justified by His grace we might be made heirs according to the hope of eternal life." Titus 3:3-7

I can't remember a time when I didn't know about God. We weren't the kind of family that was in church every time the doors were open; we didn't often all go to church together as a family; we didn't even have family prayers or devotionals. Our pattern was more off-again-on-again churchgoers. Mother would take us to Sunday School and church and sometimes Daddy would meet us. Even though in our home we never talked a lot about godly things, I always knew about God. How did that happen? I think it was my mother taking us to Sunday School and Vacation Bible School and, I believe it was the influence of my grandmothers. I had two godly grandmothers who talked about Jesus and their love for God and His Word and who must have prayed for me.

When I was nine, I began to hear God knocking on the door of my heart, calling me to Him. So one night during an invitation to accept Christ as my Savior, I gave my heart to Jesus. I promised to live for Him forever. And I meant it. I tried. But then life happened. Not knowing how to grow as a Christian or even that you were supposed to, over the years, I would draw near and fall away, draw near and fall away.

Then, as a teenager I felt a special call on my life to be in the ministry. I promised I would, and I meant it. I tried. But then I made some choices that altered the course of my life. I became rebellious. And at fifteen, I ran away from home, got married, and dropped out of school. What seemed so very exciting at the time was a formula for disaster. When I found myself and came to my senses, I believed that God certainly couldn't use me now. I had messed up the plan.

At age eighteen, I began going to church with my two small children and again surrendered my life to serve the Lord. I wanted a God-centered home and began to witness to my husband. During a Lay Witness Mission weekend at our church, he made a commitment to Christ and later felt called to the ministry. For the next ten years we served in several churches as pastor and wife. We worked hard. I taught every age of Sunday school. I organized and worked VBS. I kept the nursery. I helped the elderly. I taught community literacy classes. I cooked for college kids. I worked, worked, worked and got tired, tired, tired. I began to resent all the things that earlier had been a joy. It was all mowing without the blade down; all for the wrong reasons.

My husband and I put ourselves through college while doing college ministry. It was during that time that my life began to unravel. I can't put my finger on the exact time, but I began to drift away from God. I completely quit Bible study and prayer. I was still working for God but not worshipping Him. I was mowing without the blade down.

Following graduation, burned out, and disillusioned, we decided to leave the ministry. We wanted to make money and be successful. We turned our backs on everything we had committed to. A little window was all Satan needed, and he came roaring in, destroying everything in his path. 1 Peter 5:8 warns, "Be of sober spirit, be on the alert. Your adversary, the devil, prowls around like roaring lion seeking someone to devour." We had taken off the armor and allowed the enemy into our family.

I began to try to make up for all the "fun" I had missed by getting married so early and being trapped in religion. There was a chasm, an emptiness I couldn't fill. A degree didn't fill it. Two degrees didn't fill it. Fun didn't fill it. partying didn't fill it. I was looking for love in all the wrong places and did not find it. It seemed so cool, so exciting at the time. But looking back, it was a reign of terror. Proverbs 16:25 says, "There is a way which seems right to man, but its end is the way of death." Four short months of hell ended with a divorce and four shattered lives. Then came the guilt, shame, bitterness, and anger. The consequences for poor choices. The results of a broken family on the lives of children. The enemy always does that—leads you away from God with enticing promises, and then kicks you when you are down. When, like the prodigal in Luke 15, I came to myself again, I began to try <u>on my own</u> to put my life back together. I wasn't going to ask God for help this time. It was partly feeling disillusioned and partly feeling unworthy. I wasn't mad at God; I was just disappointed in myself and in others. It was too little too late for me.

But not for our great and loving God! It is never too late for Him.

And I am convinced that nothing can ever separate us from his love. Death can't and life can't. The angels can't, and the demons can't. Our fears for today, our worries about tomorrow, and even the powers of hell can't keep God's love away. Whether we are high above the sky or in the deepest ocean, nothing in all creation will ever be able to separate us from the love of God that is revealed in Christ Jesus our Lord. Romans 8:38-39 NLT.

God was loving me and caring for me all along the way. I just didn't know it. He was providing for and protecting my children and me. He sent people my way; he gave me a second chance for love and family with the finest person I have ever known.

My repaired life and family were good, but not "too godly." God kept calling me back to serve him, but I was having none of it. I wasn't worthy and wasn't about to make another commitment; I had failed too many times. I would simply try to keep a nice balance between my life and my faith.

I found I couldn't keep the scales balanced. Because I was trying to be in control, I kept right on with my life full of hidden guilt and shame, feeling unworthy to be in His service. I would just try hard to live a good life and attempt to make it up to God…I would try to be good enough. A few years later a friend invited us to church, and we started going. Later, I even began teaching Bible study again. Even though things looked good on the outside, no one knew the pain inside. Sadly, I discovered that the church at that time offered no help at all for its hurting members: the divorced, the single parents, the abused, the families in crises, and so many others. There was no outreach or in-reach for such folks. The church simply functioned as if the hurting didn't exist. The walking wounded had to seek help elsewhere. From experience I knew that that the world was waiting with open arms to take in the hurting with plenty of empty promises to relieve the pain. How sad that must make our Lord, who sought out such as these in his earthy ministry and commissioned us to do the same. The churches today that are growing exponentially are those who welcome and minister both physically and spiritually to the hurting and lost. I, however, didn't know such havens existed.

I had a deep, deep wound that needed the healing touch of God. I was doctoring myself instead of going to the Great Physician. I didn't know how seriously I needed God's touch. I just knew I couldn't get well.

For fifteen years I lived in a cycle of misery and mercy, functioning well and then completely defeated. Every time there was a problem, I spiraled into depression. I would berate myself for my sin. How could I have done the things I did? How could I have allowed Satan to trick me? God, I'm so sorry! It was exhausting.

Then, one day while driving my mower through life, my Heavenly Daddy called me over to Him. He asked, "What are you doing?"

I replied, "I am living."

"No you're not...you're in bondage...you don't have the blade down!"

Now, I knew I wasn't living the abundant life that Jesus had promise and had died for me to have, but I didn't know what to do. I only knew that I could not go on the way I was. I was worn out from my own efforts at happiness and survival. Finally one day, at the end of my rope, flat on my face on the kitchen floor, I begged God to help me, to heal me. He answered me immediately and a slow healing process began.

The healing for me came through Bible study and prayer. I clung to the Psalms, especially 27 *The Lord is my light and my salvation; whom shall I fear?* and 40 (David's psalm after his sin) *I waited patiently on the Lord and He inclined to me and heard my cry. He brought me up out of a pit of destruction, out of the miry clay and He set my feet upon a rock making my footsteps firm. And He put a new song in my mouth, a song of praise to our God.* And 121: *I lift my eyes up to the mountains; from whence does my help come? My help comes from the Lord.* I began to claim promises I didn't believe were true for me, and the Lord brought them to pass.

A major breakthrough occurred for me, ironically, through a series I had begun to teach at our church called, "The God of Second Chances." Realizing that Moses, David, Jonah, Peter, Mark, and others had been called to service and failed, only to be forgiven and used in a powerful way gave me hope and courage.

It was at about this time that I attended a women's retreat. I wanted to go and at the same time was terrified that I would have to deal with some deep issues. I wasn't sure that I had the energy to survive it. But I learned it wasn't about my efforts, it was about *His love*. It was there on Saturday morning in a sweet little chapel, I met my healing Savior face to face. The bonds of guilt, shame, anger, and depression were broken. I left it at the cross. I was free. Free to receive the love and forgiveness He had been waiting to give.

I had always stalled out at **remorse** and **repentance**, I'd been saying "I'm sorry" for twenty years, never moving on to **restore** and **rejoice**. It was over. I was **recommissioned** in joy. I experienced what Paul described in Galatians 5:1, *It was for freedom that Christ has set us free; therefore, keep standing firm and do not be subject again to a yoke of slavery.*

Jesus set me free. *And who the Son sets free is free indeed.* Free to live. Free to serve. Free to receive. Free to love. I am a blood-bought child of the living God; a child of the King, a princess to the Prince of peace.

Jesus, Others, You – Service – You are now freed to serve.

The next truth in our journey toward JOY is our relationship with others. We are commanded to love and serve others. We can't all be preachers or missionaries, but we can all do something. We were all blessed with gifts and talents to increase the kingdom. Jesus told his disciples that the way people would know they belonged him was by the way they treated others. *By this all men will know that you are my disciples: if you have love for one another.* John 13:35

Jesus' teachings about the attitude with which we are to serve are clear. *You shall love your neighbor as yourself.* (Matthew 22:39) *Love your enemies and pray for those who persecute you.* Matthew 5:44

What does that have to do with freedom and JOY? We cannot be free to serve if we harbor anger, hate, and unforgiveness in our hearts. And it's one of the reasons our prayers are not answered. *And whenever you stand praying, forgive, if you have anything against anyone; so that your Father also who is in heaven may forgive you your transgressions.* Mark 11:25

Love is a choice, not a feeling. It is an action and an attitude.

I've heard people say that they just can't forgive. Or they say they will forgive, but will not forget. When we think about whether we can or should forgive, let's think about Jesus--the perfect sinless Son of God, forgiving his murderers as He died. Forgiving us while we are still in our sin. Compared to other people I might not be so bad, but compared to Christ, I am not so perfect. Christian forgiveness is not "forgive and forget"; it is "remember and forgive anyway".

We are to be like Christ. But I cannot love others and forgive wrongs on my own. It's not within my natural abilities; it requires supernatural power. The only way I can truly forgive is through His power; and that is what He promises. *I can do all things through Him who strengthens me.* Phil 4:13.

Do you have unforgiveness in your heart? Toward your parents? A former spouse? Your spouse? Your children? Your boss? Co-workers? Neighbors?

Who do you need to forgive so that your relationship with God can be restored? Of whom do I need to ask forgiveness? I cannot be freed for JOY if I hate or am bitter or harbor unforgiveness.

I am not responsible for the other person's response, I'm just to obey and trust God with the results.

Jesus Owns You – Surrender – You are now free to grow and to know Him more!

This is the fourth truth. This is the <u>You to God</u> part. So what is my job now? I am saved. I love and serve others. What else is there? I must grow. I must press into Him. I must mature in my relationship with Him to experience JOY. I can't just live on prior experiences – it has to be everyday!

The longer Paul served Christ the more he wanted to know about Him and the more humble he became. He writes to the Philippians from prison with a message of joy. Joy in spite of circumstances. In chapter three he sums it all up.

*But whatever things were gain to me, those things I have counted as loss for the sake of Christ. More than that, I count all things to be loss in view of the surpassing value of knowing Christ Jesus my Lord, for whom I have suffered the loss of all things, count them but **rubbish in order that I may gain Christ, and may be found in Him**, not having a righteousness of my own derived from the Law, but that which is through faith in Christ, the righteousness which comes from God on the basis of faith, **that I may know Him**, and the power of His resurrection and the fellowship of His sufferings, being conformed to His death...not that I have already attained it, or have already become perfect, but I press on in order that I may lay hold of that for which I was laid hold of by Christ Jesus.* Philippians 3:7-12

To know Him and to be found in Him! The more I know, the more I want!

How do we grow? We grow in many ways, but these might be helpful as you begin your journey.

- Prayer – Follow the practice of ACTS (adoration, confession, thanksgiving, supplication) when you pray. Remember, prayer is communicating with God—listening and hearing, as well as speaking.

- Bible study – Start in the book of John in the New Testament, then read the other Gospels (Matthew, Mark, and Luke.) Paul's letter to the Philippians, Galatians, Ephesians, and Colossians are a great place to study the doctrine of the church. The Psalms should be a part of what you read or study every day. Find a good commentary and use it to help you understand the historical context of the scriptures.

- Meditation – Choose one to three verses of a passage and spend several days studying it deeply and thinking about it. I like to write it in my journal from several translations, write the definitions of key words from the dictionaries, look up the original meaning of words and phrases, and then meditate, asking God to show me what He wants me to learn from the passage.

- Worship and Praise – Whether in a corporate setting at church or alone in your room, Psalm 22:3 tells us that God inhabits the praises of His people. Sing to Him, tell Him how great and awesome He is. Praise Him as you would an adoring and wonderful Father.

I had a vision recently as I was worshipping with my hands lifted, and I saw Jesus facing me as His hands met mine. Blood from the nail wounds initially covered my hands as He touched His to mine; then as He folded His hands over mine, they were clean. I looked into His eyes burning with love and compassion. I leaned in, my forehead touched his, the thorns hurt as they pressed into my scalp, and then were gone. Finally, my heart was touched, and I was surrounded by his presence. It was the safest and most peaceful feeling I had ever experienced. I kept hearing Paul's words from Ephesians 4:24, exhorting me to "…put on Christ." The Savior was touching and cleansing my will, my mind, and my heart. And He does it in love.

Here is the beautiful paradox of our salvation. Christ sets us free from the slavery of sin and adopts us into His family as his own children. He bought me at the slave auction, set me free, and then adopted me as his own child. I'm not a freed slave—I'm a daughter of the King. I'm a princess to the Prince of Peace. I am the child of God. I am free, but I am only happy belonging to Him. The longer I know and serve Him, the more humbled I am because of His grace and mercy.

Paul started out his career demanding his status as an apostle; he ended up claiming only to be a bondservant of his Lord, and saying, …*Christ Jesus came into the world to save sinners, among whom I am foremost of all. And yet for this reason I found mercy, in order that in me as the foremost, Jesus Christ might demonstrate His perfect patience as an example for those who would believe in Him for eternal life.* I Timothy 1:15-16

Thinking About It

? Your Thoughts:

1. Describe a time when you felt like you were "mowing without the blade down".

2. Have you accepted the free offer to freedom? If not, you're going the wrong way. Jesus is standing at the door of your heart knocking, waiting with a gift of love for you. You have to open the door and say yes. Today is the day. Acts 2:21 says that whoever calls on the name of the Lord shall be saved. Just ask.

3. Are you bound and shackled by fear, guilt, shame, doubt, blame, sins of the flesh, anger, bitterness, depression? Do you want to be free? Jesus wants to free you! Just ask.

Go Deeper

Select from the following to begin meditating. Spend a week reading and journaling your thoughts.

1. Psalm 1:1-3

2. Jeremiah 29:11-13

3. Isaiah 61:1-3

4. Number 6:24-26

5. I John 4:7-10

6. Romans 8:1

Commit the verses you choose to meditate on to memory.

† So What?

What do you want to remember from the story? What difference does this make to you? What will you do?

_____

_____

_____

📖 Study Session

Write your thoughts about God's love and forgiveness after reading the following:

- Matthew 25:31-46 -

- Matthew 18:21-35 -

- Depict the following truths about JOY using a drawing of a cross and labeling it:
  - ➢ JOY: We are to love the Lord with all our heart, soul, mind, and strength. (Us to God)
  - ➢ JOY: We are to love others like Jesus. (Us to others)
  - ➢ JOY: We can only do both through the power He supplies. (God to us)

🕊 Praying (from Philippians 4:13)

Thank you, Lord, that I can do all things through your strength and that in You I have found freedom and joy.

_____

_____

_____

_____

Author's note: One day after reading Humpty Dumpty to one of my grandchildren, I kept hearing the cadence and rhythm of that nursery rhyme with a message. I began to write it down and the result is the following little poem. I certainly lay no claims to being a poet or a "nursery rhymist", but this silly little piece shares a tiny part of what the Lord did for me.

Whole Again

Proud Little Christian sat on a wall.
Poor Little Sinner had a great fall.
All kinds of answers and all kinds of friends
Couldn't put this one together again.

Serving and working, so proud of her place,
Wasn't God lucky He saved her by grace?
First busy, then careless, she drifted away.
"I'll do what I want! I deserve it." She'd say.

"What will it hurt? Just a little's okay."
"Everyone's doing it. Live for today!"
A tiny, small crack in the armor was all
The enemy needed to set up the fall.

The fall, oh, the fall,
From the height of the wall.
She knew she had drifted,
But the distance seemed small.

Now silent the voice of the shepherd, once clear.
Now dim was the light from His presence, once near.
How silly the ones who served him appeared;
How simple their music, how naïve their fear.

Blind to the dangers so close to the edge,
Unequipped for the battle, Forgotten the pledge
To love Him, to serve Him. no matter the cost.
Now crushed by the impact, the shame, and the loss.

Now, flat on her back, stuck and covered in muck,
She cried out to God, "I need you so much!"
"I'm broken! I'm sorry! I've tried and I've failed.
Oh, Jesus, Come heal me! My Strength and my shield."

That instant the Savior reached down from above,
His face full of mercy; His eyes full of love.
Extended out to her, a scar in each one,
His Hands, my Sweet Jesus, my Savior, God's Son

Took this heart, badly broken and crushed from the fall.
Made worse by self-efforts to fix what was ruined,
There were scars from the fall;
There were stains from the cures.

With one touch He created a new heart alive;
Not patched up or bandaged, but new with His life.
Gone the pain, gone the guilt, with no trace of the past,
By the true Great Physician, the First and the Last.

The pieces, once broken, are whole and in place
Connected by Jesus secured by His Grace.
I cannot, I will not go back to the wall
My King, my Redeemer, my Savior, My All.

No words can express the immense grace of God,
The love, peace, and the joy that comes from The Word.
So each day, each moment praise goes to the One
Who found me and healed me and loves me - my Lord.

Chapter 7

The Hurdler
Perseverance through Faith

Consider it all joy, my brethren, when you encounter various trials, knowing that the testing of your faith produces endurance. And let endurance have its perfect result, that you may be perfect and complete, lacking in nothing.
James 1:2-4

A minister friend of mine, Ken Haney, recently shared this story about perseverance. He was teaching at a small private school; they needed a girls' coach, and he was available. Now, Ken had never coached girls before, but that didn't seem to be a problem; the school needed someone to fill the position – how hard could it be? He made it through the fall and into the spring semester without incident.

During track season, Ken wanted his girls' team to have the opportunity to participate in a track meet. Knowing his team would have difficulty competing with more experienced teams; Ken carefully selected events for his girls. He found a hurdles event with only one entrant! He quickly entered one of his girls who particularly wanted and needed a medal. He told her about the race and assured her she was going to win a medal.

"But, Coach, I've never run hurdles before."

"No problem." Ken explained how simple it was, "You just run toward the hurdle and throw your front leg over and your other leg will follow. Keep your eye on the goal. Remember, you're going to at least win second place!"

The girl was determined. She had the "eye of the tiger!" She desperately wanted that medal! She prepared herself at the starting line, stretching and jogging about. Ken was quite proud of himself, knowing how much taking home a medal would mean to her. No one would ever remember that there were only two entrants. The school announcement would say "second place," not "second place of two places."

The race started and the girls took off toward the first hurdle, side-by-side. The other teams' runner gracefully cleared the hurdle while Ken's runner tumbled over, hurdle and all. She threw the front leg up but it caught the hurdle, and she went crashing forward onto the track. She went down hard scraping her hands and her knees. This wasn't one of those nice rubber tracks of today; this was an old cinder track. Ken, watched in shock, and then figured she would take herself out of the race. "Hey, nice try," he would say. But before he could move toward her, she got up, brushed herself off, focused on the finish line, and took off again. She approached the second hurdle, and with a loud groan, threw her front leg over, clearing it. Her back leg caught the hurdle and down she went again, scraping the same bloody knees and hands.

Ken was praying, "She will stop now; she tried, but she just can't do it." Before he could get to her, she again dusts herself off, faces the next hurdle, and with a steeled determination takes off. She again trips over the hurdle falling forward on her bloody, battle scars.

Ken is now watching in horror, moving toward her. Every person in the stadium is focused on the girl hurdler. The other girl has long finished the race and is waiting with her coach to receive her first place medal. But this tenacious hurdler, this girl with a vision for a second place medal, again sets her focus on the finish line and the hurdles standing in her way. She runs full-speed for the next hurdle; but instead of throwing her leg over, she slows down and pushes the hurdle over with her right foot, steps over it, and continues running. The crowd is now cheering for this pillar of perseverance as she takes down and steps over the rest of the hurdles on her way to the finish line. At the finish line she celebrates as if she had just won an Olympic gold medal.

What a lesson! What a heart! She had a goal; she wanted that medal. All she had to do was finish. She wasn't quitting until she won it, one way or the other. There's more than one way to clear a hurdle!

We need that kind of spirit. When we face the hurdles and obstacles in our lives, when we go down, bloody and scraped, we need to be able to stand and brush ourselves off, focus on the goal and take off again.

That little girl's knees healed up leaving only a small scar, which, along with a silver medal, would be constant reminders for the rest of her life of the sacrifice she was willing to make because the prize was worth it. The prize is worth it in our lives. The scars can either cause us to relive sad could-have-beens or they can be medals of honor, symbols of a fight worth waging. Don't give up; look up and get up.

What race are you faced with? What hurdles stand between you and your heart's desire? What is worth it for you? What are you willing to sacrifice in order to achieve your dream? Is it peace, happiness, money, success? Only God can fill the void in our lives and finding Him is worth everything it takes. *You will seek Me and you will find Me when you search for Me with all your heart.* Jeremiah 29:13

God has impressed this verse on my heart as I seek to know Him more. I want to know Him more; I want to seek His face.

In doing Kingdom work we have four choices as we seek Him. We must be cautious for there is only one that will be blessed. Meditate on these examples as you consider your motives for seeking Him.

➤ Doing the Wrong Thing for the Wrong Reason

- ▪ Like the religious leaders who set out to kill Jesus to protect their way of life. He was a threat to "the way it has always been." Even though they saw the miracles; they were blind to who He really was. Their fear and jealousy kept them from recognizing the One they were seeking.

- Like Judas who wanted the Messiah his way, on his terms. When Jesus didn't fit his preconceived idea of what the Savior should look like, his selfish motives drove him to betray Jesus.

➤ Doing the Wrong Thing for the Right Reason

- Like Saul, before his conversion, zealously serving God by persecuting Christians, believing he was right. He was full speed ahead going the wrong direction. God had to knock him down and blind him so that he could see the light.

- Like Peter cutting off Malcus' ear when Jesus was arrested. Peter reacted before he thought, going on emotion, as usual; he seemed willing to fight and die for his Lord at that moment. He didn't understand what kind of fight was required, even though Jesus had warned them. How amazing that only a few hours later he cowardly denied even knowing Jesus. Feelings aren't trustworthy; but truth is.

➤ Doing the Right Thing for the Wrong Reason

- Like the crowd that followed Jesus for what he could do for them. They were willing to follow as long as He was meeting their needs, making them feel good. It was an amusement to some, a fad to others. They loved the miracles. But when he called for sacrifice and commitment, the crowds thinned to the devoted few.

- Like James and John arguing about who had the better place in the kingdom. This just had to make Jesus roll His eyes! Can you imagine? Two of the top three disciples, Jesus' inner circle, arguing over who gets to "sit in the front seat." How they missed the point about His kingdom. They, as Jesus modeled, were called to serve, not be served.

➢ Doing the Right Thing for the Right Reason

- Like Mary worshipping at His feet and serving Him with a humble heart. Reckless abandon. Total and complete devotion despite tradition, gender or cultural expectations, ridicule or persecution.

- Like Paul, who suffered unthinkable hardships and persecution due to serving his Lord. Paul writes this encouragement to keep seeking, to persevere from prison,

Not that I have already obtained it, or have already become perfect, but I press on in order that I may lay hold of that for which I was laid hold of by Christ Jesus. Brethren, I do not regard myself as having laid hold of it yet; but one thing I do: forgetting what lies behind and reaching forward to what lies ahead, I press on toward the goal for the prize of the upward call of God in Christ Jesus. Philippians 3:12-14

There is an inspiring example of perseverance in Exodus chapters 32-33. When Moses came down from the mountain after receiving the law from God, he found that the people had been disobedient. God was angry with them, and Moses said that he would try to intervene for them. After Moses' intervention, God told him to go to the land they had been promised, but that He would not go with them. God said they were an obstinate people and if He went with them, He would have to destroy them. Moses was devastated and set up a tent of meeting outside the camp to pray. (Exodus 33:7-11) All those who were seeking God went there to see Moses and to pray. It is interesting that in order to see and hear God, Moses had to move away from the camp, the people, the noise, the sin. We must have a "tent of meeting" in our own walk with God, away from the noise and distractions of our crazy lives.

Moses said to God: *Let me know your ways, that I might find favor in your sight. If you don't go with us, please don't lead us from here. For how can it be known that I have found favor in your sight...is it not by your going with us so that we, I and your people, may be distinguished from all other people on the face of the earth?* Then God replied: *My presence shall go with you and I will give you rest.* (Exodus 33:13-14) God granted Moses request, not because he or the people deserved it, but because of His mercy.

But Moses wanted more. Paul might call this the "pressing in" part. Moses then asked for God to show him His glory. God told Moses, *There is a place by me and you shall stand there on the rock; and it will come about that while my glory is passing by, that I will put you in the cleft of the rock and cover you with my hand until I pass by.* (Exodus 33:21-22) He pressed in and he saw the glory of the Father.

When Moses came down from the mountain after being in the presence of God, his face shone with brilliance. (Exodus 34:29-35) The people knew he had been with God. That's what I want. I want to be so full of the Savior's love that it shows. I want people to know I've been in His presence. We are to reflect His light in this dark world. That's what our mission is on this earth—

to be light in a dark place. In order to do that we must prepare; we must soak up His light.

We have the same choice the disciples had. They were failures when they focused on themselves. They changed the world when they focused on Jesus and were filled with the Holy Spirit. We are, too, an obstinate and sinful people. And we have an intercessor better than Moses on our behalf, Jesus. My plea to God is the same as Moses! "Oh God, please! If you don't go with us, please don't let us leave this place." It is now our choice: I'm going to pitch a tent of meeting like Moses and wait to see what God does.

When our granddaughter, Beth, was a toddler, she had begun to sleep with her mom and dad after an illness. The problem for her parents was that she would not sleep in her own bed after that. They tried everything. She would start out fine, but would wake up in the night crying out for them. Her mother was exhausted from lack of sleep every night. They decided to try to ease her back into her room by letting her sleep in her own bed at the foot of their bed. Then after a while they would move her bed to her room.

Well, the first night started out fine, as usual. Then, as usual, she woke up. She first whimpered. They ignored. Then she cried. They ignored. Her requests became more definite. "Momma!" They ignored. Now, standing in her bed, looking at them in the night shadows, she screams, "MOMMA!!" Finally her exhausted mother whispered, "Beth, go to sleep." The response only encouraged her. Hopefully, she cried, "Momma, get me." They ignored. "MOMMAAAAAA!"

Her mother firmly replied, "Beth, if you don't go to sleep, I'm going to spank you." Beth was silent. Relieved that the threat has worked, they waited for her to lie down. Then they heard a quiet little voice whisper, "Daddy?"

She wasn't about to give up. She could see the object of her desire and she would persevere…whatever it took! Spiritually, we should be like Beth; with the desires of our heart before us crying out, "Abba, Father!"

Dancing on Daddy's Feet and Other Stories of God's Love

Thinking About It

? Your Thoughts:

1. What past trials or struggles have you persevered through? How has it changed you?

2. In what ways can people tell that you belong to Christ?

3. Why do Christians have to struggle?

Go Deeper

Read the book of Acts. Note the ways that the disciples and the early church had to persevere through trials and tribulations.

† So What?

What do you want to remember from the story? What difference does this make to you? What will you do?

_____

_____

_____

Study Session

➢ Write your thoughts about God's love and our perseverance after reading the following:

Mark 14:36

Romans 5:3-4

Romans 8:15

Galatians 4:6

Hebrews 12:1

🕊 **Praying** (from Exodus 32-33)

Father, Our prayer is that of Moses. If you don't go with us, please don't let us leave this place. Go before us and prepare the way for Your work. I've seen what I can do. I want to see what You will do; I want to see Your Glory! Show us Your glorious work. Keep me in the cleft of the rock--my Rock and my Redeemer, Jesus.

Chapter 8

The Stain

Come now, let us reason together, says the Lord.
Though your sins are as scarlet, they shall be as white as snow.
Though they are red like crimson, they will be like wool.
Isaiah 1:18

Have you ever made a mess and then, trying to clean it up or cover it up, you end up with a bigger mess?

I was about six years old, and we lived in a little house in Amarillo. While our Daddy went to work everyday, Mother stayed at home with the four of us, ages eight, six, three, and a new baby. I had been playing in my room and went to get a drink in the kitchen where my mother was working. Mother gave me a glass of grape juice or Kool-Aid and told me to stay in the kitchen with it. I begged her to let me take it to my room where I was playing. I promised to be careful, to use both hands, and then proceeded to show her that I could do it by myself. As I left the kitchen, I'm sure I was very careful; she was watching. As I entered the living room on the way to my room, I began to hurry. Out of her sight and feeling quite the big person, I decided I could carry it in one hand. Just as I was about to turn down the hall, the cup slipped out of my hand. It spilled on the carpet up next to Daddy's chair and down the wall. I quickly turned to see if she saw. She didn't, but I knew I was going to be in big trouble. She told me to be careful and I hadn't been. She told me to use both hands; I didn't. I thought I could do it by myself; I couldn't.

I should have called out to her that I had made a mistake; but I didn't. Instead, I tried to clean it up myself. I grabbed tissues from the bathroom and began to wipe the stain. It just spread farther. I decided the only thing to do was to cover it up. At least that would delay the trouble. In my six-year-old mind I was only thinking of covering the mess of the moment to avoid trouble; long-term consequences were never considered. I quickly grabbed my baby sister's diaper bag and placed it over the stain next to the chair. It covered most of it, but I needed more. I got a box from my room and placed it next to the diaper bag. Then I stacked some books next to the box. Deciding this all looked funny, I covered it all up with a blanket for camouflage and went to my room to play.

I completely forgot about the incident until The Voice! "What is this? Who put all this stuff here? Ginger Kay! (That was never a good sign.) Come here!" I acted like I didn't hear.

Strategy number one: Pretend to be deaf. Maybe she would go away. I was too young to know that mothers founded the FBI (Family Bureau of Interrogation.) She wasn't going away. "Come here! Right now!....Who put all this stuff here?" Now, why do they ask questions like that when they know the answer? It only makes you think you have a chance when you don't.

Strategy number two: Play dumb. "I don't know," I said with a look of shock and surprise at the blanket-covered stack.

"Did you do this?" Hum...sounded like a 50/50 chance. In that instant I decided my chances were pretty good with a "no" answer.

Strategy number three: lie and blame someone else. "I didn't do it. I don't know who did it. I guess Mike or Garre did." Hey, they weren't there and had probably done something worth being punished for that day anyway. I was actually beginning to believe it myself. The more I talked, the worse it got. I was digging a deep, deep hole.

Then, she moved the stuff. When she moved the blanket and the books and the box and the bag, she saw the stain. I hadn't just redecorated the living room; I had tried to cover up a big mess. I really don't remember what happened next. It was probably what we today call a significant emotional event; a repressed childhood trauma. It most probably involved my mother living out the scripture commanding her not to spare the rod and spoil the child. That was before children had self-esteems to worry about.

Whatever the sequence of events, Mother had to clean up my mess. How much easier for her if I'd just told her from the start. But now, instead of just a spill, there was a stain. Not just on the floor, but also on the bag, the box, the books, and the chair where I had stuffed the stain-soaked tissues. Everything I had tried to cover the mess with was stained.

This story is the story of our lives. It is the story of my life. God has a plan for our lives and knows what is best for us. But we, like children, rebellious and willful, try to do things on our own making a big mess. We slip up, goof up, trip up, mess up. Sometimes it's on purpose, sometimes just a mistake. Even when we try to live a good life and do good things, we can't. Whatever the reason, the result is the same: a stain. The Bible uses three words for the condition. The words may sound antique, but the meaning is very twenty-first century. Our **sins** (missing the mark, mistakes) and **transgressions** (getting off the path, going the wrong way) and **iniquities** (wrongs, perversions) are like stains. We are all stained. Some a little; some a lot. Some a blob; some a spot. For this bad condition there is some good news:

➤ Bad condition:

▪ It's universal. It's everyone. "All have sinned and fallen short of the glory of God." (Romans 3:23) "If we say we have no sin, we are deceiving ourselves and making God a liar." (I John 1:8) It's not about being better than the person next to you…it's about being as good as God. And we can't. Even our attempts at being religious make God sick.

▪ It's terminal. It is permanent. "The wages of sin is death." (Romans 6:23) It's like hearing from the doctor that you have a terminal heart condition and there's no human hope. A Band-Aid won't fix it. Without a transplant, a new heart, we will die. Without His mercy, we are doomed.

➢ Good news:

▪ It's fixable. There is a cure. God wants to give you a new life, not just patch up the old one. A new heart is waiting for you. He wants to remove the stain, not just cover it. "If we confess our sin, He is faithful and righteous to forgive us our sins and cleanse us from all unrighteousness." (I John 1:9)

▪ It's free. It's undeserved. We can't earn it; it is a gift that we must accept humbly, like a child. This is a stumbling block for us because we want to do it ourselves. It costs us nothing; it cost Jesus everything. He took our punishment on Himself in order to cleanse our stain. He paid off our debt. His own blood pays the bill for our heart transplant. Paul explained to a man this way "… when the kindness of God our Savior and His love for mankind appeared, He saved us, not on the basis of deeds which we have done in righteousness, but according to His mercy" (Titus 3:3-5)

▪ It's for one reason. He loves us and wants us to be His children. Not to be His slaves, but to be His children. I rejected God for years because I thought if I gave in to Him, He would take away everything I had and make me suffer.

It's like the story of the man who, like the prodigal son, had turned his back on his wealthy family and their lifestyle. Years later, he found himself roaming the streets begging strangers for money just to be able to eat. One day he touched a man on the shoulder and said, "Mister can you spare a dime?" When he saw the man's face he realized it was his own father.

His father, upon recognizing him, threw his arms around him and said, "Son, I've looked everywhere for you all these years. I've found you. You want a dime? My son, everything I have is yours." Think of it. The son was wandering around asking the world for a dime; and all the time the Father was looking for him to give him all that he had. "For God loved so loved the world, that He gave His only begotten Son, that whoever believes in Him should not perish, but have eternal life." John 3:16

As a child of six, I couldn't remove the juice stain from the myself. My mother had to do it. I knew it was a stain, I knew it was bad, but all I could do was try to cover it up with other things. We have to realize that we all have a stain on our lives. Everyone, even the nicest person you know. We must realize that we can't remove it by ourselves. We can try. We can try by going to church, by being religious, by doing good deeds. We can even compare our stain to others, and by comparison to others, it might not look so bad. We can try to get God to love us enough to overlook the stain. We can try to cover it up, to forget it, to decorate it with activity. We can try to drown it with alcohol, with fitting in, with looking for love in all the wrong places, even with knowledge. We can be very sorry for the stain, remorseful, wish it wasn't there; but that won't take it away. The more we try to fix it the worse it gets. The stain will still be there, and it will stain everything else it touches, everyone else it touches, until we let God deal with it.

God, in love, will reveal to you who you are in Him. When we see our condition as a hopeless sinner, God sees the opportunity for an extreme makeover. *If we confess our sin, He is faithful and righteous to forgive us our sins and cleanse us from all unrighteousness.* I John 1:9

You may be thinking that your stain is too bad, too big, too dark, to be forgiven. Listen to me: it is not. God loves you, no matter what. You are precious in his sight. The entire Bible is the story of God's love, pursuit, and restoration for stained people. Abraham lied to save his own neck; God loved him, forgave him, and used him. Moses was a murderer; God loved him, forgave him, and used him. David was an adulterer, then lied and had a man killed to cover it; God loved him, forgave him, and used him. Peter denied that he ever knew Jesus; he was forgiven and served Christ the rest of his life. Thomas doubted until he saw Jesus with his own eyes. The woman at the well had been married five times and had a live-in at the time of her encounter with Jesus. Before his conversion, Paul had Christians killed. No sin is so great or so small that he cannot and will not forgive if we ask. God is not like we are. He didn't send Jesus to condemn us, but to give us life.

The stain on my mother's rug may have stayed there forever as a reminder of my mistake. Maybe my mother couldn't get the stain out and, if she'd been the type, she could have reminded me of it every day for the rest of my life. That's not how God works. He's not like us or our mothers and dads and brothers and sisters and cousins and friends and neighbors and bosses who are only human and make mistakes and let us down. He knows about the stain. It's not a shock and surprise to Him. He loves us anyway and wants to cleanse us and free us. It is why He sent Christ to redeem us.

Wherever we are, He is chasing us. He wants us. He is waiting. A song by Phillips, Craig, and Dean says it this way:

He'll do whatever, whatever it takes.
His grace reaches lower than your worst mistake.
And His love will run farther than you can run away.
He'll do whatever it takes.
(From *He'll Do Whatever it Takes. Favorite Songs of All* album, Phillips, Craig & Dean, Star Song Records, 1998)

And He has already done whatever it takes. Sometimes in my head I can still hear my Granny's scratchy voice singing this old hymn that says it so clearly:

Jesus paid it all,
All to Him I owe.
Sin had left a crimson stain;
He washed it white as snow.
(Elvina Hall, 1865)

What about you? Do you need that kind of hope? Are you walking through the living room of your life trying to do it all by yourself? Have you made a big mess of your life? Are you trying with everything you can find to cover it up? Listen to me: you can't make it right without Jesus! But, you can turn to Him today and cry out, "Jesus, save me!" And I promise you, He will.

Do you need to ask God to undo your mess? He will. You can ask Him to cleanse you and give you a new heart. You may be thinking, "Well, I'm really a great person. I've never done anything really that bad. I live in America, go to church, I'm not as bad as others. I think I'll just take my chances. After all, God is love." God doesn't measure like we do. It's all the same to God: lies, gossip, murder, pride, idolatry. I'm not asking you to get religious; please don't! It's not about religious rules and do's and don'ts; it's about a relationship with Jesus Christ. It's about having a face-to-face meeting with the Savior and saying, "yes" to Him. You can't be good enough; you can't be too bad. You can't try harder and hope that in the end it will all just be okay. There is only one way. It is up to you.

If you want to turn your life over to Him, you can pray this prayer, believing it in your heart:

> "Jesus, I know I'm a sinner and need your forgiveness. I now turn from my sins and ask You into my life to be my Lord and Savior. Forgive me my sins and give me Your gift of eternal life. Thank you for dying for me and saving me."

If you prayed that prayer and meant it, you are saved and have begun a wonderful journey as one of God's children. If you begin to doubt it, read this story again and just thank Jesus for what he did for you!

What can wash away my sin?
Nothing but the blood of Jesus.
What can make me whole again?
Nothing but the blood of Jesus.
Oh precious is the flow that makes me white as snow.
No other fount I know.
Nothing but the blood of Jesus.
(Robert Lowry, 1876)

Now, go tell someone! Paul, the apostle, said that nothing could keep him from sharing this message of hope about Jesus:

I am not ashamed; for I know whom I have believed and
am convinced that He is able to guard that which I have entrusted
to Him against that day
.2 Timothy 1:12

Thinking About It

? Your Thoughts:

1. Was there a time when you made a big mess and someone else had to clean it up?

2. What does the sacrifice of Christ mean to you?

3. Do you know people who are lost and don't know what they are looking for? Who are going around begging for a dime, like the man in the story?

Go Deeper

Read Luke 15.

Describe what each of these parables teaches about God.

The lost sheep –

The lost coin –

The lost son –

† So What?

What do you want to remember from the story? What difference does this make to you? What will you do?

_____

_____

_____

_____

✣ **Praying** (from Romans 5:8)

Thank you, Lord, for demonstrating your love toward us, while we are still sinners, by dying for us.

_____

_____

_____

_____

FAITHFULNESS

GENTLENESS

SELF-CONTROL

Welcome In The Name of Christ

The Least of These

He Sent my Brother

Wide-Right

But when the Holy Spirit controls our lives, he will produce this kind of fruit in us: love, joy, peace, patience, kindness, goodness, faithfulness, gentleness, and self-control.
Galatians 5:22 NLT

Chapter 9

Welcome in the Name of Christ

Do not neglect to show hospitality to strangers, for by this some
have entertained angels without knowing it.
Hebrews 13:2

"Welcome in the name of Christ."

That's what the sign on my front door says. But, do I really mean it? Or, do I mean, "Welcome in the name of Christ some of you?" Or, "Welcome in the name of Christ when I'm in a good mood?" Which is it?

I just hate those mirror experiences…you know the ones where you have to take a good look at yourself, and it isn't pretty.

When we claim to be a Christian, we are held to a different standard. "By this all men know that you are my disciples if you love one another." (John 13:35 NIV) The enemy will use any opportunity to destroy your reputation, to taint your image, and to discourage your witness. When we do not show the love of Christ in everything we do, every minute of the day, we are open to the enemy's attack.

Not long ago, on a cold wintry Saturday morning, my doorbell rang. It was already one of those days…you know the kind…nothing was quite working out. I was watching three of my grandchildren, who were not getting along with each other. I was on the phone counseling a friend who was in crisis and who needed to talk longer than I had the time for. I was already running behind for the day…I needed to be working on a Bible lesson I was preparing to teach.

In between crying children, a crying friend, and me still in my pajamas because I hadn't had time to clean up and get ready, the doorbell rang. All three kids ran screaming, "I'll get it!" I looked outside and didn't see a car. That only means one thing…kids selling candy or candles for school or a politician wanted a vote. Trying to keep little munchkins from escaping from under my legs, I barely opened the door to see a cold junior high age girl, bundled up and holding a coffee can with a hole cut in the top.

She politely, yet firmly, explained that she was collecting for third world hunger for a nearby church. There had been some recent scams in our neighborhood, and I was leery. My first thought was, "Yea, right! A bunch of kids going around duping people out of money for drugs." I looked into her eyes and believed she was honest. But, I was too busy.

With fussing, crying kids under my feet and my friend on hold, I politely told her I was too busy right now. Could she come back later? Now, isn't that the internationally understood code for, "Don't Come Back?" I shouldn't feel bad…after all, I give to my church and to lots of other things. I can't give to everything! I was relieved that that was over…and, after all, I didn't say "No"… I just postponed. Right? Wrong!

Ten minutes later, the doorbell rings. Three little voices sing out, "I got it!!"

"No, don't answer it," I whispered. "Let's just let them go away."

"Why, Mammaw? Are they strangers?" my little angel of guilt asked.

"Just because." I answered, waiting to hear them leaving my yard, with three sets of questioning eyes on me.

A moment of silence, then…a loud, strong knocking on the door. She said she'd be back, and this determined little missionary meant it! Okay! Okay!

I opened the door to the young girl, who now had two backup guys. They were looking me over. Two of the grandchildren were still fussing and trying to get around me to see who was at the door. I saw the other one down the hall climbing from a stool onto the kitchen cabinet heading for the cookies I had hidden.

"We're back. You said come back later and here we are. Would you like to make a donation?"

Unbelievable! "Look guys…today's just not a good day. Thank you, but not today." I said closing the door.

"Couldn't you just give something?" She pleaded, leaning her face into the door opening as I tried to close it.

"Not today."

"Not even $2.00?" She pleaded through the tiny crack.

"No, not today!" I said firmly, closing the door. Good grief!

Immediately I felt rotten. And it bothered me all day. Why couldn't I have just stopped for one minute and found some change or something for these kids?

The Holy Spirit continued to bring the incident to my mind. I couldn't get the image of her pleading eyes through my closing doorway out of my mind. "Not even $2.00?" I should not only have given an offering, I should have included hot chocolate and some encouragement.

That evening in our worship service, I was struggling to worship. I kept seeing that face. I prayed, "Oh, God, please don't let my sinful actions discourage those kids who are trying to make a difference for you."

And then something flashed in my mind—an image. I remembered the inscription on my doorknocker we had recently placed right above the doorbell: "Welcome in the Name of Christ." Tears of remorse streamed down my face. Realization, Remorse, and Repentance. Three of the four big Rs...I realized what I had done, I was truly sorry, and I confessed it to the Lord, repenting of my attitude and actions. But, I knew I still had to deal with the fourth R: Restitution. God clearly let me know I needed to try to make it right and ask for forgiveness. I remembered the name of the nearby church and determined that the very next day I would go to the church and make a small anonymous donation.

God said, "No, you won't...that would be easy. You're going to do the hard thing. You're going to go to the church, talk to the leader, confess, and make a large donation." I intended to do it the next day, but got busy and never took an opportunity to do so. A day soon became a week. Every morning in my quiet time, I was reminded of my task. How could I expect God to bless my ministry for Him until I went to those I had offended? I knew I could not wait any longer to visit with the youth pastor and explain.

I went by the church and introduced myself to the youth pastor. After explaining the situation to him, he said, "Wow…I'm blown away! I…I…can't believe you are here. I already knew about it. After the kids went out, we gathered back here and talked about the day. They told me about you and some other experiences they had." Oh, My! I was on their prayer list!

I told him I wanted to make a donation and asked him to pass along my apology to the kids. He gratefully took my donation, paused, and then said, "I feel like the Lord really wants you to tell them, not me. It will mean more if they hear it from you."

Oh, my! He was right. I knew I must, but it's never easy to confess in front of those we've offended. That next evening the youth group had a scheduled meeting, and I was the agenda. As I was introduced, I looked out over the faces of these young searching souls thanking God for them; that they were here, seeking a relationship with Him and not on the streets looking for what the world has to offer. I spied the little missionary who had been at my door; she was sitting with her arms folded in near defiance, giving me "the look." I shared what the Lord had taught me through this, then asked their forgiveness, and left them with the following challenges.

➢ **Be faithful.**

God will bless your efforts to obey Him. When God called Jeremiah, he was very young and afraid of what others would think. God assured him that youth was not an excuse to avoid the call of God and that it didn't matter what anyone thought as long as he obeyed God. Jeremiah 1:7

➢ **You are not responsible for the results**.

God is and He's better at it than we are. People may not respond the way we want or on our time schedule. Only God knows the outcomes He chooses to accomplish. Jesus had just commissioned Peter to a great task and Peter's response was, "What about John? What's going to happen to him?" Jesus in a very clear way explained to Peter that that was really none of his business. He was to focus on what he was supposed to do. John 21:20-22

➢ **Don't judge Christ by Christians**.

We are all human, even when we belong to Him. We all sin and make mistakes. It's why Jesus came to save us! Romans 7

Realize that people do have bad days, off days, down days. **Be kind and show the love of Christ to them**. Luke 6:35-38

They were forgiving and even shared some of the other "bad people" stories they had experienced that morning. I did feel somewhat relieved that I wasn't the worst! But then I thought about that doorknocker again and what it represented.

These are some of the lessons I learned from the incident as I reflected:

➤ In every thing that happens and everyone God brings into your life, look for ways to bless, to minister, to encourage.

> *Conduct yourself with wisdom toward outsiders; making the most of the opportunity. Let your speech always be with grace, seasoned, as it were, with salt, so that you may know how you should respond to each person.*
> Colossians 4:5-6

➤ If you're going to nail God's name on your house, stick a fish on your car, and wear a cross around your neck, you'd better be ready to live out your faith at all times.

> *...walk in a manner worthy of the calling with which you have been called*
> .Ephesians 4:1

> *Conduct yourself in a manner worthy of the gospel of Christ...*
> Philippians 1:27

➤ Remember what Jesus said about children and the meek: *I tell you the truth, unless you change and become like little children, you will never enter the kingdom of heaven. Therefore, whoever humbles himself like this child is the greatest in the kingdom of heaven. And whoever welcomes a little child in my name welcomes me. But if any one causes one of these little ones who believe in me to sin, it would be better for him to have a large millstone hung around his neck and to be drowned in the depths of the sea."* Matthew 18: 3-6

Thinking About It

? Your Thoughts:

1. Describe a time when you were disappointed by the words or actions of a Christian.

2. Has there been a time when you have not represented our Lord well? When you have caused others to stumble or doubt?

3. Should Christians be held to a different standard in the workplace and community than others are?

Go Deeper

Read Matthew 5-7, known as the *Sermon on the Mount*, everyday for one week. Read it from several translations.

→ What does Jesus teach about the following:

Salt and light

Love and hate

Prayer

Giving

Forgiving

Worry

Judging others

The narrow and broad way

Wise and foolish builder

→ Select five verses to commit to memory.

✝ So What?

What do you want to remember from the story? What difference does this make to you? What will you do?

🕊 Praying (from Romans 5:8; Luke 9:48)

Thank you, Father, for teaching me lessons through my mistakes and for loving me in spite of the things I do and say. Thank you for demonstrating your love for me while I was still a sinner, by sending Christ to die for me that I might know You. Teach me to be more like Jesus, to receive others in His Name as He receives me.

Chapter 10

The Least of These

And whoever receives one such child in My name receives me, but whoever causes one of these little ones who believes in Me to stumble, it is better for him that a heavy millstone be hung around his neck, and that he be drowned in the depth of the sea.... See that you do not despise one of these little ones, for I say to you, that their angels in heaven continually behold the face of My Father who is in heaven. Matthew 18:5-6, 10

Let the children alone and do not hinder them from coming to Me; for the kingdom of heaven belongs to such as these. Matt. 19:14

Death and life are in the power of the tongue. Proverbs 18:21

Think of the power we possess when we open our mouths to speak! We either build up or tear down...people, things, events. James said that with the same mouth we bless God and curse men, and that it shouldn't be that way. (James 3:10) I can recall actual words spoken to me over forty years ago that affected the way I think about myself and others. What a responsibility we have as Christians to speak words of blessings to build up those around us. What a huge responsibility we have to speak the truth in love and yet, carefully guard our words. Ephesians 4:15

I recently experienced one of the greatest blessings of my life while I was on a visit to an elementary school to observe a couple of teachers. I had to leave the school that day because I was weeping. It was not because I was sad or because someone had hurt my feelings. It was because I was so overwhelmed by what I saw and heard. I was so moved by the compassion of a teacher that I could not stop crying.

When I arrived at the school early that morning, I observed a teacher, who I know to be a Christian and a fine teacher, standing in the hall talking to a little girl. This girl was the most pitiful sight I had ever seen. She was dirty, her hair was matted, and the clothes were filthy and worn and were several sizes too large. Her expression as she looked up into the face of this teacher was hopelessness and sadness.

As I walked past this scene, my heart immediately ached for the child and for the teacher, who looked exhausted and frustrated. As if teaching under normal circumstances isn't exhausting enough, this was the day before the big state test that students have to pass, and the pressure is overwhelming. All I heard of the conversation were the teacher's strong words, "Not today, Kid!" I did not hear the rest of the conversation, but I worried that in her frustration this teacher might say or do something that would devastate this child, and without intending to, leave a lasting scar.

The reason the feeling was so strong for me that day was that just a few days before a dear friend had shared her story of just such a lasting scar inflicted by a teacher. Here is her story in her own words:

I remember it like it was yesterday. I was in the second grade—the ripe old age of seven. Our class was lining up to go to the cafeteria and have our group picture made. My teacher, Mrs. H, was busy going up and down the line trying to get us in order. As she approached me, I figured she would move me to the back of the line because I was so tall. Instead, she leaned down and with hatred said, "You don't even have your hair brushed today;" then she moved me to the back of the line. I didn't know if she moved me because of my height or because of my hair. I don't remember anything else about that moment—the class picture—but I'm sure I nervously pushed down my hair and tried to look decent. What Mrs. H didn't know was that that comment never left me.

Who knows why I didn't have my hair brushed—it could have been any number of reasons. Evenings were not always calm at our house, making the mornings tough sometimes. Maybe the night before my dad had been so drunk that he yelled and screamed at my mother for hours and we girls had a hard time sleeping through his yelling while my mom was locked in the bathroom. Maybe he was so drunk that he started beating her up so badly in front of my sisters and me that one of us called the police and maybe they were there a while before they took him to jail for the night. How nice and quiet those nights were. Or, maybe the night before I had started crying when we went to bed, like so many times before, and I couldn't stop. I would cry because I would worry that my mom would die and we would just have my dad, and I knew that wouldn't work, and, so, I would cry wondering what would happen to me and my four sisters. I slept with two of them every night—two in one twin bed, three in the other. One of the sisters would eventually go get my mom and she would come and assure me that she wasn't going to die. I would finally go to sleep.

Who knows what had happened the night before so that the morning was hard and I wasn't able to get my hair brushed.

You can see why my first thought for that little girl in the hall that day was, "Oh, Lord, I pray that this is not a moment for this little girl like it was for my friend almost forty years ago." The years, a successful life, and loving family had not removed that scar from my friend's tender heart. I wondered how many of those moments that little one had already had in her life.

I spent the rest of that day observing teachers and students, but couldn't get the picture of that child out of my mind. Near the end of the day I decided I needed to find the teacher and share my concern with her. Arrogantly, I decided I needed to warn her about life-long scars left by our careless words. I ran into the teacher as she was hurrying down the hall with a group of children; I told her I wanted to talk to her about the conversation with the little girl that morning. But before I could share my concerns, she beamed and said, "Oh, yes! And you should she her now!" Confused, I asked what she meant. She told me a little about the girl and asked if I wanted to hear the rest of the day's story. Of course I did.

She explained how this child was being raised by an overwhelmed and under-prepared single father. She was left to care for herself and often had to get herself and her siblings to school while her father worked night jobs or shift work. She had already missed ten days of school since Christmas and this wasn't the first time she had shown up in this condition. The teachers had collected clothes for this girl before; but they seemed to get lost, never being worn back to school.

But this morning was different. She told me she had a glimpse of that child that she had never had before; the pressures of testing, and homework, and schedules was suddenly in perspective. The little girl appeared at school early that day and said (what I couldn't hear as I observed that morning), "Teacher, you said to be here this week and get a good night's sleep and eat a good breakfast so we can do well on the test. I am here, but couldn't find anything to wear and we don't have anything to eat."

The teacher said to the little girl, "Not today, Kiddo! You're not going to school like that today." So, this kind passionate teacher sent her student teacher to Wal-Mart to buy clothes while she and the school nurse took the girl, washed, dried, and curled her hair and cleaned her up before the teacher let her go to class. She wanted that little girl to have this one day to remember; to remember that for once she mattered to someone. The teacher did what a caring mother would have done for this child in the name of Jesus. She said upon entering class, the students all remarked about how beautiful she looked. For the first time in that child's life she heard kind words from her peers that others take for granted.

What an angel of mercy that teacher was. What a defining moment for that little one. How I pray that it will always be remembered when the other moments in life come. I pray she will always know that at least one person cared, thought she was beautiful, and beleived she was worth it…even on the busy stressful day before state testing. And that person was a teacher. Thank you, Tina.

Then the King will say to those on His right, " Come you who are blessed by my Father; take your inheritance, the kingdom prepared for you

since the creation of the world. For I was hungry and you gave me something to eat, I was thirsty and you gave me something to drink, I was a stranger and you invited me in, I needed clothes and you clothed me, I was sick and you looked after me, I was in prison and you came to visit me." Then the righteous will answer him, "Lord, when did we see you hungry and feed you or thirsty and give you something to drink? When did we see you a stranger and invite you in, or needing clothes and clothe you? When did we see you sick or in prison and go to visit you?" The King will reply, "I tell you the truth, whatever you did for one of the least of these brother of mine, you did for me.
Matthew 25:34-39

I was sharing this story with a group of first year teachers in a workshop hoping they would carefully consider the power their words and actions have over the lives entrusted to them. Following the session, a young lady waited until everyone else was gone to speak with me. She told me she liked the story, and I thanked her. She moved closer and said more assertively, "No, I mean I <u>really</u> like that story. I think you should tell it to every group of teachers you have. It's very important." I realized that this wasn't a compliment, but an impassioned plea. I looked in her eyes brimming with tears and said, "You were one of those little children, weren't you?"

"Yes, I was. And I wouldn't be here today if a teacher had not stood up for me." Since that day, I tell this story to every group I have. Almost every time, someone else comes forward after the session or writes me sharing a similar experience, either the abuse that my friend endured or the advocacy of a compassionate teacher in their life like my friend, Tina.

Thinking About It

? Your Thoughts:

1. With which person in the story can you best relate and why?

2. Who has God placed in your path to lift up or build up?

3. Who are your "least of these?"

Go Deeper

Read the following passages and meditate on applying Jesus' teachings:

Matthew 24:42 – 25:46

Matthew 18:1-14 -

Mark 9:30-37

Mark 10:13-16

Luke: 9:46-56

2 Corinthians 1:3-5

James 1:26-27

James 3:1-12

Select five verses to commit to memory.

✝ So What?

What do you want to remember from the story? What difference does this make to you? What will you do?

_____

_____

_____

🕊 Praying (from Isaiah 61:1-3; Luke 4:18-19)

Thank You, Lord, that You came to bring good news to the afflicted, to bind up the brokenhearted, to proclaim liberty to the captives, and freedom to prisoners. Thank You for coming to give recovery of sight to the blind; for setting the downtrodden free. Thank You that You comfort all who mourn, that You give beauty for ashes, oil of gladness for mourning, and a mantle of praise for fainting.

_____

_____

_____

_____

Chapter 11

He Sent My Brother

If anyone wishes to come after Me, let him deny himself, and take up his cross, and follow me.
Matthew 16:24

One of the most embarrassing moments in my life was the day the A-team was selected in ninth grade girls' basketball. We had a coach with a vision—build a team and win the state basketball championship--every year. It was his second year to coach at our school where his task was to take a bunch of silly girls who had never learned to play, never won, never been challenged, and transform them into athletes.

Before he came the standard had been, "You girls play, have fun, and don't hurt yourselves." He was different. He was demanding. And, he did win. He won the first of many state championships the next year, his third year there. He continued to hold that vision and in doing so established a standard for girls athletics that continues to this day, some thirty-nine years later.

He had standards—high standards and expectations. Everyone understood the expectations. There were no excuses. It was hard. It was consistent. It was fair. It was understood—if you wanted to play on his team, you had to pay the price: hard work, commitment, and dedication.

At the end of the prior year's season in my eighth grade year, I had quit the team. I left athletics. I convinced the principal to change my schedule. I was just an average player anyway, and I didn't like all the rules and regulations. Besides, I had other plans for high school that would not allow me to play basketball. Well, I ended up being miserable. The PE class I had been assigned to was learning to square dance! I wanted back in athletics—I wanted back on the team. I wanted to be back with my friends.

The administrative decision was that I would have to wait until the next year, and then I could sign up. So, I did. I never talked to the coach; I never explained; I just showed up with all my friends expecting to make the team with no questions asked. The coach asked me what my plans were for high school, and I told him I wasn't planning to play basketball all four years—I had other plans—cheerleading. I just wanted to play this year. Nothing else was said. Workouts began. I had a lot of catching up to do, and I worked hard. Then, the day came for dividing up the group into teams. This really meant choosing those who would play and those who would not play. We all knew it. The purple and the white.

We were in line formation, and the coach began walking up and down each line with his clipboard in hand, calling out names to go over to the other side. After a couple of names, it was clear that he was calling out all the top players. He came to my row. He called out the girl in front of me. He passed me over and called out my good friend behind me. As she left the line for the other side, she said, "Come on, he called you." Now, I knew he hadn't. But in that hopeful, mindless, adolescent moment, I went for it. Maybe I could sneak in, and he would never know. Maybe he would <u>think</u> he had called me and would let me stay. He called a few more girls. Then, everything stopped. The gym went silent. The only sound was his gym shoes as he walked over to me and said, "Ginger, go back over there. I did not call your name."

In front of everyone, I walked back over to my place in line in complete silence, except for the sound of my gym shoes on the wooden floor. All eyes were on me, most in pity, all in shock. All glad it wasn't them.

I stayed in athletics that year and played on the B-team second string. He never said another word to me about it.

I shall never forget that day. I was so embarrassed. I thought he hated me, and that was why he didn't choose me. He didn't hate me; he just had to do what he said he would do. He could not change the standard because I had changed my mind. He could not put me on a team when I was not committed to the cause or to the team or to the vision or to the coach. I just wanted to be with the people who were committed until the next year offered something else that I wanted to do. I never accepted his leadership nor committed to his standard. I wanted all that went with being a part of a championship team without any of the obligations.

The other girls were committed and passionate. Being the best at basketball was the desire of their hearts, and they dedicated themselves to the cause. The following year, those girls went to state and won. I was there, on the sideline, with the crowd. I can say I was there; I can say our school won; but, I cannot say I played; I cannot say I have a trophy; I cannot say I was on a championship team because I was not willing to make that choice and commitment.

That experience is a portrait of what God expects from us when He calls us. That's what Jesus was saying to Peter in John 21. "What are your plans, Peter? How much do you love me?"

☑ When God calls, He expects a total and complete commitment to Him and to the cause.

☑ There is no offer of part-time, when-convenient, for-a-season discipleship. It's all or none.

☑ You can't sneak in! It doesn't matter who your friends are, who your parents are, how talented you are, or how determined you are.

☑ The call to serve requires a commitment to the cause (the Kingdom), the process (discipleship), and the person (God). Some want to commit to one without the others, but with God, there are no "deals".

☑ God doesn't hate those who don't choose Him and His Way. He just has to do what He said He would do. He has done everything to provide a way.

He doesn't hate us—He loves us…so much that He gave His Son as the sacrifice for our sins so we could be with Him.

I remember a time when my parents had told me that I go to a particular place with my friends, but I went anyway. Everyone else got to go, and I wanted to have some fun, too. Of course, my parents found out and my mother called and told me to come home. Emboldened by the distance between us and by my friends encouraging me, I refused. I told my mother I wasn't coming home, maybe ever. She relayed my answer to my father and he ordered me to come home. Again, I refused. I kept right on doing what I was doing. It wasn't very long before I looked up and saw my older brother. My father had sent my brother to get me. He told me I needed to come home. I knew I did, but now I was afraid to…afraid of what was waiting for me. We did not talk back to our parents without consequences. I knew I was going to get it!

My brother began to explain how worried and upset my parents were. I expected him to tell me how stupid I was, but he didn't. He convinced me to come back home with him. On the way home, he "instructed me in my ways." He gave me a good talking to. He told me that my parents didn't hate me when they disciplined; that they loved me. My parents' anger was because my behavior was unacceptable, and they loved me too much to let me destroy myself. When we arrived home, I was expecting to be killed. As we entered the house, my brother stepped ahead of me in front of my father and said, "Go to your room. I'll talk to Daddy." I will never forget that night as long as I live. My brother intervened for me so that my relationship with my father could be restored. I don't know what he did or what he said, but the next day, things were right with my parents. I still had the consequences to pay for my dumb choices, but the relationship was right. My father loved me so much that he sent his son to get me so I could be with them again. They waited for me to come home.

That's a picture of our God. That's what He did for us. "For God so loved the world, that He gave His only begotten Son, that whoever believes in Him shall not perish, but have eternal life."(John 3:16) Our Savior came to get us and stands before our Father making us right with Him. He provides the way; He is the Way.

This is how God showed His love among us: He sent His one and only Son into the world that we might live through Him. This is love: not that we loved God, but that He loved us and sent His Son as an atoning sacrifice for our sins. Dear Friends, since God so loved us, we also ought to love one another.

I John 4:9-11

Thinking About It

? Your Thoughts:

1. Was the coach fair? Was he just? Have you experienced a time when you thought God was unfair? How did you face it?

2. Describe a time when someone intervened on your behalf to prevent you from being punished or from being harmed.

3. What life experience have you had that provides the best picture or example of God's love and protection?

Go Deeper

Read the following:

John 10:7-18

Matthew 20:28

John 3:13-18

John 6:35-58

Romans 5:6-11

Galatians 4:4-5

Ephesians 1:7

I Timothy 2:5

I Peter 1:18; 3:18

Select five verses to commit to memory.

✝ So What?

What do you want to remember from the story? What difference does this make to you? What will you do?

_____

_____

_____

📖 Study Session

Write your thoughts about the commitment God expects after reading the following:

Matt 22:37-40

Matt 16:24

Matt. 7:21-23

John 1:12-13

John 14:21

🕊 Praying (from Isaiah 64:8; Psalm 36:5)

Thank you, Father, for being a good and righteous King. Thank you for being our Father. We are the clay, You are the potter; We are the work of your hands. Your loving kindness, O Lord, extends to the heavens; Your faithfulness reaches to the skies.

Chapter 12

Wide Right

Love is patient, love is kind, and is not jealous; love does not brag, and is not arrogant, does not act unbecomingly; it does not seek its own, is not provoked, does not take into account a wrong suffered, does not rejoice in unrighteousness, but rejoices with the truth; bears all things, believes all things, hopes all things, endures all things. Love never fails…Now abide faith, hope, love, these three; but the greatest of these is love.
1 Corinthians 13:4-8,13

I first met Stephen when I spoke to the faculty of the enormous high school. He served as one of two associate principals for a student body of over three thousand and a faculty of about 250 with seven assistant principals under his supervision. During the morning session, before I even knew who he was or what his position was, I noticed him. For one thing, he is almost seven feet tall with a striking presence and attractive features.

He was also an ideal participant—laughing at the right times and unashamedly wiping tears from his eyes during a touching story. At breaks and discussions, he was a magnet; people were drawn to him. His leadership ability and the respect of his colleagues were evident.

We sat down to lunch with Stephen and the other associate. After the introductions and small talk, I looked at him and asked, "What's your story? What brought you here?" For the next hour I was blessed to hear about his life journey and in doing so, learned more about the love of our great God.

Stephen was a star athlete and scholar for a school in Texas that expected to win the state championship in football every year. Football was the community culture, and it drove academics and politics. He had planned to play college and then professional football, basketball, or baseball. He was a star in each. As the team's quarterback his senior year, one of his two defining moments came during the state semifinal game. After a tough fought battle, his team scored a touchdown as time ran out to tie the game. This was in the years before high school teams played overtime to break a tie. Ties were broken based on the stats. The other team was ahead in the tie-breaking statistic: penetrations inside the opponent's twenty-yard line. The extra point attempt would determine which team went to the state final and which team went home. For most of the seniors, it would be the final game of their lives. For seventeen-year-old Stephen, it felt like life and death; you see, he was also the extra point kicker. If he made the kick, they won; if he missed, they went home. With screaming spectators and no time on the clock, the holder took the snap and placed the ball as Stephen booted it. It looked good, it looked good… and then faded off to the right. He missed it <u>wide right</u>.

The expected responses occurred on both sides: ecstasy for the winners and agony for the losers. Having lost games before Stephen knew it wouldn't be easy and especially with this one so close to the state championship; but Stephen said that as a young person, he never imagined the response that he personally was about to experience. Some of his own fans booed him as he left the field. Some threw things.

Before boarding the bus for the solemn journey home, his head coach called him aside. This good man who had been Stephen's coach, mentor, and friend waited until everyone else was gone and then he put his arm around Stephen and told him how proud he was of him. He told him that it was an honor to work with such a fine young man and dedicated athlete. He wanted Stephen to know that the game wasn't lost because of his missing the kick. That kick just happened to be the last play of a game in which Stephen and his teammates played well. No one person was responsible. He then added that he wanted Stephen to know that things might get pretty rough for him at school and in the community, but that he should remember what the coach had just said. He should hold his head high. The coach then bowed on a knee and prayed for him and thanked God for him.

Stephen said that act of love and compassion was what got him through the next days and weeks. His family received obscene calls, trash was thrown in his yard, and most hurtful, two of his coaches never spoke to him again after that game. He said it was then that he decided he would teach and coach. He wanted to be the one to make a difference in the lives of others, like his mentor coach had done for him.

My heart was about to burst from the emotion of this story when Stephen said, "Then came baseball season..." They were in the playoffs and guess who the pitcher was? Stephen. And he was having a bad game. He had just walked in a run, when the stands started chanting, "Wide right! Wide right!"

It was then that he experienced his second defining moment that year. As he was gathering himself to pitch, he saw his father--also a formidable figure--stand up in the crowd and walk over in front of the chanters. He stood there a minute then held up his hands as they quieted and said, "That's enough! Stop it." The chanting stopped. Stephen's team lost the game; but it was an awesome victory for Stephen who watched the man he loved more than any other in the world take a stand in his defense. Stephen said he determined that day that he would always do that; he would always stand for the right thing and stand up for those who could not stand up for themselves. And that's what he does on a daily basis for hundreds of teachers and students.

As I've reflected on Stephen's story, I couldn't help but see a picture of Jesus on the cross with his outstretched arms saying, "That's enough…it is finished." He stood in the gap between heaven and hell so that we could have access to the Father. I want to do that for those that God places in my path. I want to be like Jesus and stand up for those who cannot stand for themselves, even before a chanting crowd. I want to stand in the gap.

In Ezekiel 22:29-30 after the Lord lists the sins of Israel, he especially targets those who are supposed to protect others,

The people of the land have practiced oppression and committed robbery, and they have wronged the poor and needy and have oppressed the sojourner without justice. And I search for a man among them who should build up the wall and stand in the gap before Me...but I found no one.

He found no one so He came Himself to stand in the gap for us. Isaiah 59 – 61 prophesies the coming of the Messiah. When Jesus stood up to read in the synagogue some 700 years later, he used part of this prophecy to define himself and to describe His mission.

The spirit of the Lord God is upon me,
Because he has anointed me to <u>bring good news to the afflicted</u>;
He has sent me to <u>bind up the brokenhearted</u>,
To <u>proclaim liberty to captive</u>,
And <u>freedom to prisoners</u>;
To proclaim the favorable year of the Lord,
And the day of vengeance of our God.
To <u>comfort those who mourn</u>,
To grant those who mourn in Zion,
<u>Giving them a garland</u> instead of ashes,
The <u>oil of gladness</u> instead of mourning,
The <u>mantle of praise</u> instead of a spirit of fainting.
So they will be called oaks of righteousness,
*The planting of the Lord, **that He may be glorified**.*
Isaiah 61:1-3

His mission is our mission.

> *Blessed be the God and Father of our Lord Jesus Christ, the Father of mercies and God of all comfort; who comforts us in all our affliction so that we may be able to comfort those who are in affliction with the comfort with which we ourselves are comforted by God. For just as the sufferings of Christ are ours in abundance, so also our comfort is abundant through Christ.* 2 Corinthians 1:3-5

Read 2 Corinthians 1:3-5 again and underline the word *comfort* every time you see it. God comforts us through our hurts, sorrow, and brokenness and then uses those healed hurts to allow us to comfort others. It is a pay-it-forward system. Do unto others. We are his hands and feet.

A friend brought me a small gift back from a women's retreat she had attended in Oklahoma City. As I opened the small velvet pouch, I found an angel lapel pin. The pin was silver with purple glass forming the body of the angel. I wondered at the gift, especially since my friend knows that I'm not much of a jewelry person. "It's lovely," I said.

She smiled and said, "I didn't get this for you because it's jewelry, but because of the story."

The pins and other jewelry are fashioned by the dear ladies of the Methodist church that is located across the street from Murrow Building in Oklahoma City. The same explosion that destroyed that building and the lives of so many people and changed our nation forever, also shattered the beautiful stained glass windows of their church. But instead of wallowing in the tragedy, these saints gathered up the broken pieces and made something beautiful out of the shattered glass. They made angels, and sold them to raise money for the new stained glass windows. Beauty from ashes!

That angel pin is my most prized piece of jewelry. It represents everything I believe about God and love and what He asks us to do. He redeems our broken shattered lives and makes something brand new out of them, something beautiful! He then uses us to build His kingdom.

Praise the Lord!

Thinking About It

? Your Thoughts:

1. Stephen had two defining moments as a young man that shaped his life. He chose to let those events make him better. How have your defining moments shaped your life?
2. For whom do you stand in the gap?
3. How do you show the love of God to those around you at work and at home?

Go Deeper

Read I John and look for the number of times love is mentioned. Meditate on I John 3:11-18.

Select five verses to commit to memory.

† So What?

What do you want to remember from the story? What difference does this make to you? What will you do?

_____
_____
_____

🕊 **Praying** (from Isaiah 40:26-31)

Thank you, Father. You do not become weary or tired; Your understanding is inscrutable. You give strength to the weary, and to him who lacks might you increase power. Even though I grow weary and tired and stumble, I gain new strength when I wait on You. I will mount up with wings like eagles; I will run and not get tired; I will walk and not grow weary. Your way is blameless; Your word is tried. You are a shield to all who take refuge in You. For who is God, but the Lord? And who is a rock, except our God!

_____

_____

_____

_____ _____

Thanksgiving

I am thankful to God for so many people and events that He placed in my life and allowed me to experience; both the pleasant and the painful. Without those experiences, I would never have known Him and trusted Him as I do. It is my heart's desire to be able to see His face and hear Him say, "Well done."

Many people have heroes who have touched their lives in powerful ways. I can't say I have any heroes except the men and women in the Bible whose stories have changed my life. I would like to serve God with the passion that Esther did; so committed to her dangerous mission that she could say, "If I die, I die."

I long to be so passionately committed to Christ to be able to say as Paul did (from prison) in Philippians 3

Rejoice in the Lord...

Whatever things were gain to me, those things I have counted as loss for the sake of Christ. More than that, I count all things to be loss in view of the surpassing value of <u>knowing Christ Jesus</u> my Lord for whom I have suffered the loss of all things, and count them but rubbish in order <u>that I may gain Christ</u>, and <u>may be found in Him</u>, not having a righteousness of my own derived from the Law, but that which is through faith in Christ, the righteousness which come from God on the basis of faith, <u>that I may know Him</u>, and the power of His resurrection, and the fellowship of His sufferings, being conformed to His death; in order that I may attain to the resurrection from the dead. Not that I have already obtained it, or have already become perfect, but I press on in order that I may lay hold of that for which also I was laid hold of by Christ Jesus.

I am especially thankful for my godly husband and best friend, Tommy; my beautiful daughter, Amy and her family, Marvin, Richard, Bailey, Ryan, Spencer, and Olivia; my wonderful son, Chuck and his family: Amy, Alizabeth, Ben, and Gracie. I am thankful for my parents, Odell and Betty LaGrone, who provided a warm and safe home for us in times of plenty and in times of want. I love you. For my brothers, Mike and Garre, and my sister, Judy and their families: I love you all. For my precious, loving mother-in-law, Peggy, and my other sisters, Kim, Kris, and Terre and their families, I love you. And, for my best friends, my sisters-in-Christ: Anne, Darla, Marilyn, Jeanette, Karen, and Lou, I love you. For other special friends and relatives who have been Jesus to me: Cora, Tommy, Louise, Vicki, Brenda, Aunt Ann, and Shirley. For Lesli and my other Christian family at work: I love you all; it is a joy to work with such great people. Kim Beth, I especially thank you for editing and making suggestions. Although they are all gone, I am so thankful for my four grandparents; I have nothing but precious memories of them and legacies I have received from them – the love of stories, music, games, children, food, books, and the Word.

Biographical Sketch

Ginger Tucker is a former classroom teacher and education specialist. Since 1996 she has owned her own consulting company, providing training for school, business, and church personnel. She presents at local, state, and national education conferences and speaks at churches and at women's and couple's events. She is currently the Executive Director of Curriculum and Professional Development for a school district. Ginger's education includes a bachelor's degree in history and English education from Hardin Simmons University, a master's degree in history and geography from West Texas A&M University, and a mid– management certification from WTAMU. Ginger is married to Tommy Tucker and has two grown children and eight grandchildren. Her published works include *The Heart of a Teacher: Sailing the High Cs; Saving Our Greatest Resource: Helping New Teachers Succeed; First Year Teacher Notebook and Resources;* and *Dancing on Daddy's Feet and Other Stories of God's Love.*

Ginger's professional mission is to provide quality training and services in a way that enhances people's morale and performance so that they can make a difference in the lives of others. Her personal passion is to use the time and energy she has to reach the world for Christ Jesus and to leave a legacy of faith to her family.

It is a trustworthy statement, deserving full acceptance, that Christ Jesus came into the world to save sinners, among whom I am foremost of all. And yet for this reason I found mercy, in order that in me as the foremost, Jesus Christ might demonstrate His perfect patience, as an example to those who would believe in Him for eternal life. Now to the King eternal, immortal, invisible, the only God, be honor and glory forever and ever. Amen.
I Timothy 1 15-17

Dancing on Daddy's Feet and Other Stories of God's Love

Ordering Information

DANCING ON DADDY'S FEET AND OTHER STORIES OF GOD'S LOVE
1-49 COPIES   **$15.00 EACH**
50-99 COPIES   **$13.00 EACH**
100+ COPIES –   **CALL FOR PRICING**

METHOD OF PAYMENT:
☐ **BILL MY ORGANIZATION (PO ENCLOSED)**
☐ **CHECK ENCLOSED**
☐ **CREDIT CARD: VISA OR MC NUMBER** _ _ _ _ _ _ _ _ _ _ _ _ _ _ _ _ _
EXP.DATE_____/_____
CREDIT CARD SIGNATURE_____

MAIL OR FAX YOUR ORDER TO:
GKT CONSULTING, INC.
3536 MARSH PLACE
AMARILLO, TEXAS 79121
PHONE: 806-353-7291   FAX: 806-353-7526
EMAIL: GKTUCKER@MSN.COM.

YOU MAY ALSO DOWNLOAD FORMS AND INFORMATION AT
WWW.GINGERTUCKER.COM.

Name	
Address	
City, State, Zip	
Phone	
E-mail	
Organization	
Position / Title	

Ginger and Dad
1956